BUILDING
WOOD AND RESIN
RIVER-STYLE TABLES

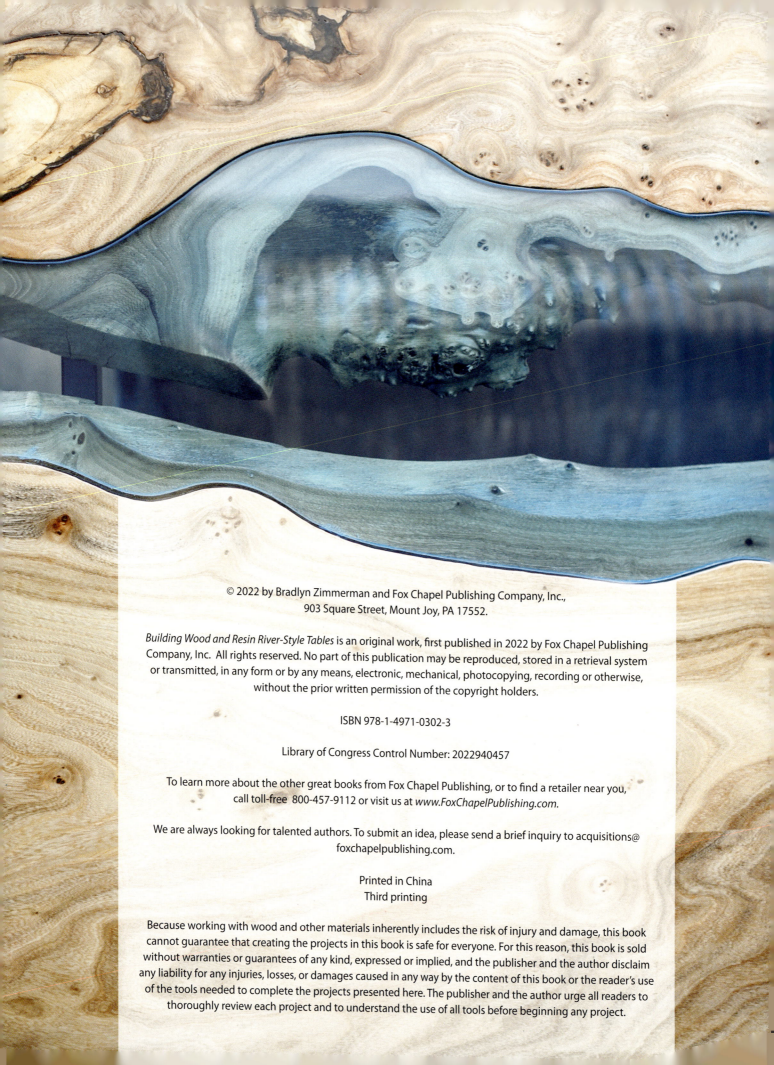

© 2022 by Bradlyn Zimmerman and Fox Chapel Publishing Company, Inc., 903 Square Street, Mount Joy, PA 17552.

Building Wood and Resin River-Style Tables is an original work, first published in 2022 by Fox Chapel Publishing Company, Inc. All rights reserved. No part of this publication may be reproduced, stored in a retrieval system or transmitted, in any form or by any means, electronic, mechanical, photocopying, recording or otherwise, without the prior written permission of the copyright holders.

ISBN 978-1-4971-0302-3

Library of Congress Control Number: 2022940457

To learn more about the other great books from Fox Chapel Publishing, or to find a retailer near you, call toll-free 800-457-9112 or visit us at *www.FoxChapelPublishing.com*.

We are always looking for talented authors. To submit an idea, please send a brief inquiry to acquisitions@foxchapelpublishing.com.

Printed in China
Third printing

Because working with wood and other materials inherently includes the risk of injury and damage, this book cannot guarantee that creating the projects in this book is safe for everyone. For this reason, this book is sold without warranties or guarantees of any kind, expressed or implied, and the publisher and the author disclaim any liability for any injuries, losses, or damages caused in any way by the content of this book or the reader's use of the tools needed to complete the projects presented here. The publisher and the author urge all readers to thoroughly review each project and to understand the use of all tools before beginning any project.

BUILDING
WOOD AND RESIN
RIVER-STYLE TABLES

A Step-by-Step Guide with Tips, Techniques, and Inspirational Designs

Bradlyn Zimmerman

Fox Chapel
PUBLISHING

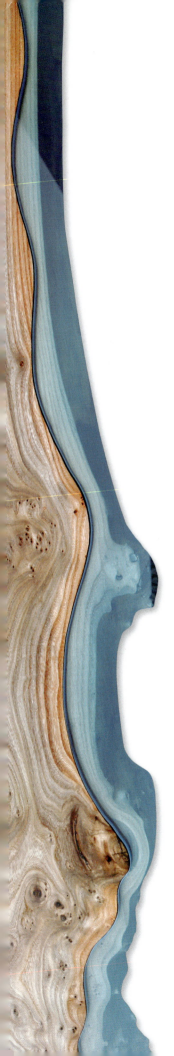

Table of Contents

Introduction 6
Overview of Building a River-Style Table 8
Gallery 10
Tools and Materials 66
Safety 70

CHAPTER 1
Introduction to Live Edge Furniture 71

CHAPTER 2
Selecting Live Edge Slabs 74

CHAPTER 3
Preparing Live Edge Slabs for Pouring Epoxy 77

CHAPTER 4
Making an Epoxy Table Form 84

CHAPTER 5
Preparing and Coloring Epoxy 90

CHAPTER 6
Pouring a River-Style Table 93

CHAPTER 7
Cutting, Sanding, and Machining the Tabletop ... 102

CHAPTER 8
Making, Mounting, and Finishing Table Legs 113

CHAPTER 9
Finishing the Tabletop 122

About the Author 126
Photo Credits 126
Index 127

82

90

74

78

102

86

97

117

122

Introduction

I began crafting river-style tables in the early 2010s as a hobby. Pretty soon, that hobby expanded into a thriving business. Sharing my craft with customers has been a great joy over the years, and I am excited to now share it with a wider audience.

Often, people are somewhat intimidated by the prospect of working with epoxy, building a mold, and the other things that go along with building a river-style table. But it is much easier than it seems. In this book, I use methods that are great for a beginner, using materials and tools readily available at any local hardware store.

I will walk you through the steps to make your own one-of-a-kind river-style table. We will cover everything from start to finish, including an introductory history of live edge furniture, how to source and select live edge slabs, mixing and coloring your epoxy, and of course, constructing your table. Once we are done, you will have a functional piece of art that you created with your own two hands!

While completing the projects in this book will take a great deal of care and attention to detail, I wanted to make sure that they are approachable to beginners. I know that most people do not have a shop full of specialty, professional-grade tools and that start-up costs can quickly get expensive. For that reason, I have kept simplicity in mind. We will be using only the most essential tools. Even if you do not own so much as a hammer, this book is designed to keep your costs at a minimum.

In this book, I will cover creating a coffee table, dining table, and end table. No matter which project you decide to tackle, keep in mind that these chapters outline how I make river-style tables. There is no singular "right" way. These are just the ways I found work best for me after a decade of making river-style tables. Feel free to experiment and make the table your own. As long as you adhere to the basic concepts taught in this book, you cannot go wrong!

Above all else, remember to have fun!

– Bradlyn Zimmerman

"The workshop to me always means great atmosphere, working, smell of wood, dust and, at the end of the day, you've created something."

- DAVID LINLEY

Overview of Building a River-Style Table

While there are many steps to creating a river-style table, the overall process can be summed up by the timeline below. Once you get started, you'll be surprised at just how quickly you create a beautiful, unique finished product!

Prepare the Slabs

Remove bark

Cut your board

Create your vision

Mix and Pour Epoxy

Let epoxy set in container

Add color and mix

Pour into river

Make Table Legs

Cut lumber to size and shape

Drill counter sink holes

Install metal inserts in bottom of table

8 Building Wood and Resin River-Style Tables

Build the Form

Apply sheathing tape

Caulk a barrier

Add end boards

Sand the Tabletop

Start with belt sander

Orbital sander, 80-grit

Smooth with progressively higher grits

Finish, Buff, and Mount Legs

Apply oil to table surface

Buff surface

Secure legs

Overview of Building a River-Style Table

Gallery

In this book, you will find step-by-step instructions to building your own one-of-a-kind river-style table. But the tables detailed within are not the only ways to make a river-style table. This gallery showcases works from artisans that you can use for inspiration when crafting your own table. Best of all, each of these pieces can be made using the concepts taught in this book!

Bradlyn Zimmerman | TheOleWoodShack
Pennsylvania, United States

I started my business, TheOleWoodShack, as a side hobby in my dad's workshop. At the time, my dad and I made handcrafted wood chairs for my uncle's furniture company. In the early 2010s, we started making a few live edge tables. With the scrap cutoffs, I started making shelving and other small pieces. These sold surprisingly well. After a few years, I began making live edge river-style tables and selling them to clients. I am thankful that I have been able to turn my hobby into a successful business. It brings me great joy to share this craft with my customers, and now, you!

The Berkshire Table
This table was created by using two slabs of cedar. The curving design on these slabs allowed us to encase epoxy on the edges, giving the table a beautiful, flowing effect. With all the cracks and decay in these slabs, we needed to carefully make sure they were all perfectly filled to create a smooth finish for the law office that is now its home.

Dimensions: 108" x 48" (274.3 x 121.9cm)
Tabletop: dark cedar
Epoxy Coloring Method: mica powder
Leg Construction/Material: steel X-beam
Finish: hardwax oil

Vegas Mesa

For this table, our client selected two beautiful slabs of claro walnut. We then coordinated the epoxy color to match the chairs and tie the whole dining set together.

Dimensions: 120" x 48" (304.8 x 121.9cm)
Tabletop: claro walnut
Epoxy Coloring Method: mica powder
Leg Construction/Material: steel base
Finish: hardwax oil

Bradlyn Zimmerman | TheOleWoodShack

Misty Blues
Figured maple is one of my favorite woods. The way the wood shimmers as the light moves across it is stunning. This wood paired with a blue river is a style that fits perfectly together.

Dimensions: 96" x 42" (243.8 x 106.7cm)
Tabletop: figured maple
Epoxy Coloring Method: mica powder
Leg Construction/Material: Z-style steel base
Finish: hardwax oil

Pacifica

Working with our client on this table, we selected some slabs from a slab supplier in Massachusetts. Then, in Pennsylvania, we transformed the slabs into the table it is today, adding waves and movement between the two maple slabs. From there, the table went to its home in California near the Pacific Ocean.

Dimensions: 72" x 48" (182.9 x 121.9cm)
Tabletop: figured maple
Epoxy Coloring Method: mica powder and white dye
Leg Construction/Material: steel base
Finish: hardwax oil

Bradlyn Zimmerman | TheOleWoodShack

Black Onyx
This small dining table is perfect for any home. Black epoxy along with black walnut always gives a classic look to fit many home styles.

Dimensions: 60" x 48" (152.4 x 121.9cm)
Tabletop: black walnut
Epoxy Coloring Method: mica powder
Leg Construction/Material: steel base
Finish: hardwax oil

Jackson Teal
Our client was looking for a unique black walnut desk. After visiting my live edge supplier, we settled on two slabs with beautiful crotch figuring, giving this desk a one-of-a-kind beauty.

Dimensions: 50" x 36" (127 x 91.4cm)
Tabletop: black walnut
Epoxy Coloring Method: mica powder
Leg Construction/Material: U-style steel base
Finish: hardwax oil

Welke Walnut
This was one of the first large river-style tables we made. In building the table, we learned the challenges of moving such a large slab with only two people!

Dimensions: 108" x 48" (274.3 x 121.9cm)
Tabletop: black walnut
Epoxy Coloring Method: solid black dye
Leg Construction/Material: handcrafted steel
Finish: hardwax oil

Englander

Black walnut is a popular choice for river-style tables. This table, along with a matching bench, makes a beautiful dining set. The large knot in the dining table slab creates a flowing river that stuns along with the character in the wood!

Dimensions: 72" x 42" (182.9 x 106.7cm)
Tabletop: black walnut
Epoxy Coloring Method: mica powder
Leg Construction/Material: V-style steel base
Finish: hardwax oil

Bradlyn Zimmerman | TheOleWoodShack

Texas Maple
In this table, we did a smoky gray epoxy color. By adding just a touch of black pigment, the result was a faint gray hue moving throughout the epoxy.

Dimensions: 72" x 48" (182.9 x 121.9cm)
Tabletop: maple
Epoxy Coloring Method: mica powder
Leg Construction/Material: steel hexagon base
Finish: hardwax oil

English Elm
To start with this table, we worked with a sawmill in Massachusetts and found a set of elm with lots of flowing grain patterns. Adding a deep teal blue makes it a one-of-a-kind dining set.

Dimensions: 84" x 42" (213.4 x 106.7cm)
Tabletop: English elm
Epoxy Coloring Method: mica powder
Leg Construction/Material: U-style steel base
Finish: hardwax oil

Anderson Gray

This river-style table has a unique coloring in the epoxy. The client wanted the epoxy to match his cabinets, so we used the same paint code and added it with the epoxy.

Dimensions: 84" x 42" (213.4 x 106.7cm)
Tabletop: black walnut
Epoxy Coloring Method: dye
Leg Construction/Material: steel base
Finish: hardwax oil

Bradlyn Zimmerman | TheOleWoodShack

Vibrant Blue
This table uses mica powder to create a bright blue effect in the river. Coupled with the variations of light and dark in the maple slabs, it has a striking effect!

Dimensions: 72" x 40" (182.9 x 101.6cm)
Tabletop: maple
Epoxy Coloring Method: mica powder
Leg Construction/Material: 3" x 3" (7.6 x 7.6cm) steel square tube
Finish: hardwax oil

Pittsburgh Steel
Metallic gray epoxy can be used with most any wood. This client from Pittsburgh chose some sturdy steel legs to go along with the gray epoxy look.

Dimensions: 72" x 42" (182.9 x 106.7cm)
Tabletop: beech
Epoxy Coloring Method: mica powder
Leg Construction/Material: U-style steel base
Finish: hardwax oil

Figured Maple Ice
Figured maple has beautiful live edges. To preserve that beauty, we used transparent tint to give the river some color, but not so much that the burls and knots in the live edge were hidden from view.

Dimensions: 84" x 42" (213.4 x 106.7cm)
Tabletop: maple
Epoxy Coloring Method: tint dye
Leg Construction/Material: H-style steel base
Finish: hardwax oil

Mappa Coffee
Mappa burl is a species of poplar. Its high number of burls is what makes it unique. This piece was especially thick, which adds to the depth of the epoxy and the overall look of the piece.

Dimensions: 50" x 30" (127 x 76.2cm)
Tabletop: mappa burl
Epoxy Coloring Method: mica powder
Leg Construction/Material: steel base
Finish: hardwax oil

Gallery

Bradlyn Zimmerman | TheOleWoodShack

Claro Walnut Credenza
Our client was redoing the entrance area of their house—including a desk, credenza and cabinet. They wanted the live edge slab to flow from the credenza into the cabinet. So, we poured a slab long enough to make doors for both the credenza and the cabinet at once. After they cured, we cut them into doors.

Dimensions: 70" x 32" x 20" (177.8 x 81.3 x 50.8cm)
Credenza: claro walnut
Epoxy Coloring Method: mica powder
Finish: hardwax oil

Green Emerald
This slab had a large void on one side. Instead of filling that with the same color as the river, we mixed up some solid black epoxy to give some contrast to the void and showcase it in a different color.

Dimensions: 84" x 42" (213.4 x 106.7cm)
Tabletop: black walnut
Epoxy Coloring Method: mica powder
Leg Construction/Material: 3" x 3" (7.6 x 7.6cm) steel square tube
Finish: hand-rubbed oil

Walnut Beam
For this table, we did everything as we normally would. We made sure to get slabs large enough that there would be enough excess wood to create a 4x4 beam to finish out the look of this modern farmhouse-style table.

Dimensions: 96" x 42" (243.8 x 106.7cm)
Tabletop: black walnut
Epoxy Coloring Method: mica powder
Leg Construction/Material: X-style steel base with wood beam
Finish: hardwax oil

Triangle Black Walnut

For this table, we made a more unusual shape than the typical rectangle. Along with that, we paired it with some slim, curving brushed-steel legs for an elegant touch to this piece.

Dimensions: 38" x 38" (96.5 x 96.5cm)
Tabletop: black walnut
Epoxy Coloring Method: mica powder
Leg Construction/Material: aluminum
Finish: hardwax oil

Bradlyn Zimmerman | TheOleWoodShack

Nokon Walnut
The client for this table was looking for a blue, but with a touch of purple to make this piece a bit different. After several mixtures of mica blues and purple, we achieved the shade that they were looking for.

Dimensions: 84" x 48" (213.4 x 121.9cm)
Tabletop: black walnut
Epoxy Coloring Method: mica powder
Leg Construction/Material: steel
Finish: hardwax oil

Walnut Waves
Our client was looking for a timeless, classic river-style table to add to their home. The end result was this gorgeous black walnut dining table featuring a blue river.

Dimensions: 60" x 48" (152.4 x 121.9cm)
Tabletop: black walnut
Epoxy Coloring Method: mica powder
Leg Construction/Material: steel
Finish: hardwax oil

Gallery

Bradlyn Zimmerman | TheOleWoodShack

Lava Canyon
This table was built for a functional sit/stand desk. The shades of yellow, orange, and red make this lava river eye-catching and unique.

Dimensions: 60" x 42" (152.4 x 106.7cm)
Tabletop: black walnut
Epoxy Coloring Method: mica powder
Leg Construction/Material: adjustable base
Finish: hardwax oil

Marble Claro
This table was made using two unique marbled claro walnut slabs. Paired with a smoky semitranslucent epoxy, we were still able to showcase the beautiful live edges on these slabs.

Dimensions: 84" x 48" (213.4 x 121.9cm)
Tabletop: claro walnut
Epoxy Coloring Method: tint dye
Leg Construction/Material: steel X with wooden beam
Finish: hardwax oil

Black Walnut Coffee Table

A coffee table like this one is the perfect piece to start out with. Easy to handle, low cost, but still very functional.

Dimensions: 30" x 20" (76.2 x 50.8cm)
Tabletop: black walnut
Epoxy Coloring Method: mica powder
Leg Construction/Material: V-style steel base
Finish: hardwax oil

White Waterfalls

The waterfall edge is one of my favorite touches when you want to add something different to a piece. It is one of the more technical parts of a table like this, but when finished will make it a statement piece in any room. In this book, you will be shown how to make this exact table.

Dimensions: 60" x 42" (152.4 x 106.7cm)
Tabletop: maple
Epoxy Coloring Method: mica powder
Leg Construction/Material: U-style wooden leg
Finish: hardwax oil

Bradlyn Zimmerman | TheOleWoodShack

Cedar Kitchenette
To give this kitchenette a rustic touch, we selected two smaller slabs so we were able to leave the live edge on for the added natural flowing-edge look.

Dimensions: 60" x 42" (152.4 x 106.7cm)
Tabletop: dark cedar
Epoxy Coloring Method: mica powder
Leg Construction/Material: wooden trestle base
Finish: hardwax oil

Classic Chic
The maple in this table lends a rustic look to this piece. A black epoxy river was used to also give it a modern feel and to complement the aesthetic of this kitchen and dining area.

Dimensions: 88" x 42" (223.5 x 106.7cm)
Tabletop: maple
Epoxy Coloring Method: dye
Leg Construction/Material: X-style metal legs
Finish: hardwax oil

Buckeye Burl
Buckeye burl is one of the few woods that naturally has gray sections throughout it. To preserve this piece, we encased it in epoxy to secure it and make it a functional table.

Dimensions: 54" (137.2cm) diameter
Tabletop: buckeye burl
Epoxy Coloring Method: mica powder
Leg Construction/Material: custom handcrafted base
Finish: hardwax oil

Southern Dining
Since this table was 72" (182.9cm) wide, we were able to encase one solid slab in the center. Then, on the edges, we added a touch of wood to complete the look.

Dimensions: 72" (182.9cm) diameter
Tabletop: big leaf maple
Epoxy Coloring Method: mica powder
Leg Construction/Material: steel
Finish: hardwax oil

Bradlyn Zimmerman | TheOleWoodShack

Cottonwood California
Cottonwood is overlooked sometimes for tables. It does require some extra finish to protect the wood, but is a cheaper option to start out with when doing epoxy work.

Dimensions: 60" x 48" (152.4 x 121.9cm)
Tabletop: cottonwood
Epoxy Coloring Method: mica powder
Leg Construction/Material: steel X with wooden beam
Finish: hardwax oil

Beach House Maple
These slabs of maple have spalting in them. It's the first step of rot in wood but does not affect the strength of the wood. Spalting leaves little black lines running throughout the wood, giving it unique patterns.

Dimensions: 60" x 42" (152.4 x 106.7cm)
Tabletop: maple
Epoxy Coloring Method: mica powder
Leg Construction/Material: steel 3x3 metal
Finish: hardwax oil

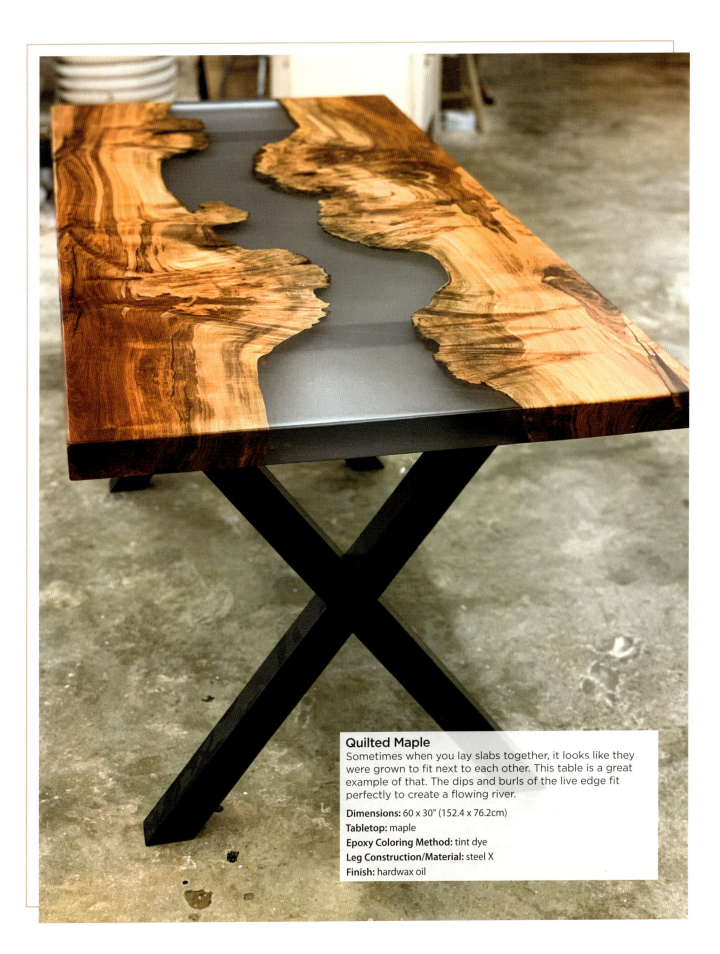

Quilted Maple

Sometimes when you lay slabs together, it looks like they were grown to fit next to each other. This table is a great example of that. The dips and burls of the live edge fit perfectly to create a flowing river.

Dimensions: 60 x 30" (152.4 x 76.2cm)
Tabletop: maple
Epoxy Coloring Method: tint dye
Leg Construction/Material: steel X
Finish: hardwax oil

Bradlyn Zimmerman | TheOleWoodShack

Seashell Cove
This slab had a natural crotch where two limbs split apart. With a layer of sand and some seashells, this makes a perfect table for a lake house.

Dimensions: 50" x 40" (127 x 101.6cm)
Tabletop: maple
Epoxy Coloring Method: clear epoxy with sand and seashells
Finish: epoxy

Ocean Shores
This simple end table adds lots of character in a little space. In this book, we will show you how to make this exact table!

Dimensions: 28" x 28" (71.1 x 71.1cm)
Tabletop: maple
Epoxy Coloring Method: mica powder with white dye
Leg Construction/Material: U-style steel legs
Finish: hardwax oil

Walnut Trestle

A black walnut and black epoxy top paired with matte black steel legs is a look that fits into many home styles, adding some rich color to the room.

Dimensions: 84" x 42" (213.4 x 106.7cm)
Tabletop: black walnut
Epoxy Coloring Method: dye
Leg Construction/Material: steel trestle
Finish: hardwax oil

Stoney Brook

This is the third table we will show you how to build. It simulates a stony creek you may find in the woods with water-washed pebbles inside the shores of some black walnut.

Dimensions: 48" x 24" (121.9 x 61cm)
Tabletop: black walnut
Epoxy Coloring Method: clear with river rocks
Leg Construction/Material: metal
Finish: hardwax oil

Gallery

Christopher Forcenito | CFWoodworksLLC
New Jersey, United States

Growing up, I was always intrigued by art and creativity. So, in 2019, I decided that I needed a hobby. I set out to make myself a river-style table. I completed my first table with success and was inspired by its beauty and the self-fulfillment that I felt with this piece of furniture and art. Curious, I posted my table on Facebook Marketplace to see if anyone would be interested. Within hours, I received dozens of likes and countless comments. I sold the table two days later to a woman who was going to gift it to her husband.

I then created a Facebook and Instagram showcasing my tables. I also post videos of my process to create them, which I believe are enjoyable to watch. I have been extremely busy ever since I began promoting my tables online, making everything from coasters to dining room tables. I take extreme pride in each piece that is put out, and I pay attention to every detail. This is more than just woodworking; this is art!

Maple Dining Table
This table was special because the river was completely clear. You are able to see directly through the table into the floor, which gives it an amazing look. The legs were custom welded iron in an X pattern and powder-coated matte. This table now lives in Lincroft, NJ

Dimensions: 144" x 48" (365.8 x 121.9)
Tabletop: maple
Epoxy Coloring Method: clear epoxy
Leg Construction/Material: X-style iron base
Finish: wood wax

Baja Blue

This is the largest table we have ever created. This table's river was Baja blue pigment, which is our most popular color. It now lives in Freehold, NJ.

Dimensions: 192" x 40" (487.7 x 101.6cm)
Tabletop: black walnut
Epoxy Coloring Method: pigment
Leg Construction/Material: custom trestle
Finish: hardwax

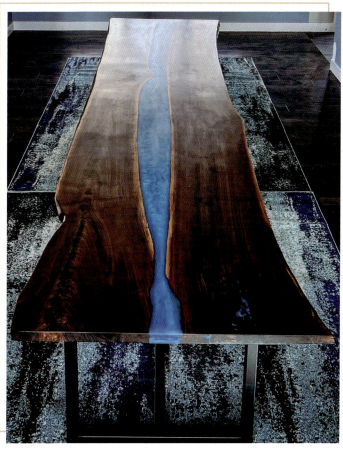

English Walnut Swirl

This table's river was a shadow gray pigment. One way we make our tables come alive is by adding depth and creating the appearance of movement in the epoxy. To do this, we utilize a swirling technique. We wait twenty-four hours until the epoxy is in a gummy state. Then, we mix the epoxy, creating swirls, which yields this effect when it hardens.

Dimensions: 144" x 48" (365.8 x 121.9)
Tabletop: English walnut
Epoxy Coloring Method: mica powder
Leg Construction/Material: X-style iron base
Finish: wood wax

Gallery

David Shaw | The Northern Joinery
Ontario, Canada

David Shaw is the owner/operator of The Northern Joinery. With his works being widely touted as functional furniture art, his contemporary, unique style and ability sets The Northern Joinery apart from other conventional woodshops. At a young age, David developed a passion for woodworking, and he still carries that same passion and drive with him today. He is constantly looking for ways to innovate and push the boundaries of conventional furniture with unique designs, building one-of-a-kind pieces for his client.

Spalted Maple Credenza
Our signature waterfall credenzas pair perfectly with a matching resin table. These pieces are both organic and contemporary. We like to think of them as functional art.

Dimensions: 84" x 25" (213.4 x 63.5)
Tabletop: spalted maple
Epoxy Coloring Meth: black dye
Leg Construction/Material: steel
Finish: hardwax oil

Mappa Burl Vanity

This mappa burl vanity is a great example of two ways resin can be used. Not only is there a blue river running through the vanity and the mirror to add to the aesthetics, but with the burl being very soft, we stabilized it with a method we call resin bathing.

Dimensions: 60" x 23" (152.4 x 58.4)
Tabletop: Austrian mappa burl
Epoxy Coloring Method: mica powder
Finish: hardwax oil

David Shaw | The Northern Joinery

Black and Gold Table
The black gold table is a great example of both a large singular pour as well as using a different-colored resin post cure to create the veins. This technique uses two very different resins, one that's very reactive with a short pot life and another with a very low viscosity and very long pot life.

Dimensions: 144" x 44" (365.8 x 111.8cm)

Tabletop: spalted maple

Epoxy Coloring Method: black dye and gold mica powder

Leg Construction/Material: steel tube base

Finish: natural oil

Ibrahim Guler | Artist and Founder of Jehoel's Works
Istanbul, Turkey

Jehoel's Works began as a hobby. While I had found some success in my entrepreneurial endeavors, I wanted to evaluate and continue the next part of my life by taking my hobby and making a profession out of it. I wanted to make personalized productions that were unique and made people feel special. I made the decision to set up a small workshop. Then, that small workshop grew. Now, it's an art village on roughly 33,000 square feet (10,000 square meters) of land.

Over time, we have made special productions for end-user designers and architects in about 30 countries. Wood is a very special material. It is good for people. You feel good when you touch it. The combination of wood and epoxy turns into a unique painting with the artist's interpretation of nature and art. When our hands work with our minds and hearts, people feel it. We produce all parts of the products we make ourselves. We use our epoxy that we produce as Jehoel Chemical with our own recipe. We ensure that every piece is special and produced with our own hands.

Ocean Waves
This river-style table employs several techniques, the most striking being the wave/surf effect created by spreading a white dye throughout the colored epoxy.

Dimensions: Approx. 144" x 44" (365.8 x 111.8cm)
Tabletop: epoxy
Epoxy Coloring Method: dye and mica powder
Leg Construction/Material: U-style wooden leg
Finish: hardwax oil

Colorful Epoxy Table

This table blends several colors between spalted hardwood. This effect is achieved by concentrating the pigment in localized sections and blending the edges together. A mixing stick is used to create the swirls throughout.

Dimensions: Approx. 144" x 44" (365.8 x 111.8cm)
Tabletop: epoxy and hardwood
Epoxy Coloring Method: mica powder
Finish: hardwax oil

Ibrahim Guler | Artist and Founder of Jehoel's Work

Shore Table
This table uses epoxy and natural materials to create a shore on the edge of the hardwood slab.

Dimensions: Approx. 84" x 48" (213.4 x 121.9cm)
Tabletop: epoxy, hardwood, natural materials
Epoxy Coloring Method: dye and mica powder
Leg Construction/Material: steel X
Finish: hardwax oil

Ibrahim Guler | Artist and Founder of Jehoel's Work®

Island Oasis
This table uses the traditional ocean effect, but with a twist. A stump is used to create a towering island with its own beach made of sand and natural materials.

Dimensions: Approx. 48" x 48" (121.9 x 121.9cm)
Tabletop: epoxy, hardwood, and natural materials
Epoxy Coloring Method: dye, mica powder, natural materials
Leg Construction/Material: unknown
Finish: unknown

Realistic River
Similar to the Island Oasis, this table uses sand, sawdust, and small plants to create a realistic river effect.

Dimensions: Approx. 84" x 48" (213.4 x 121.9cm)
Tabletop: epoxy, hardwood, and natural materials
Epoxy Coloring Method: dye and mica powder
Leg Construction/Material: unknown
Finish: unknown

Floating Driftwood

This table is completely clear, giving the effect of floating driftwood in an epoxy river.

Dimensions: Approx. 144" x 44" (365.8 x 111.8cm)
Tabletop: epoxy and olive wood
Epoxy Coloring Method: clear
Finish: hardwax oil

Ibrahim Guler | Artist and Founder of Jehoel's Work

Forking River
This table uses clear epoxy to remain see-through and showcase the characteristics of the wood edges. The slabs are positioned in three locations to create a forking river effect.

Dimensions: Approx. 144" x 44" (365.8 x 111.8cm)
Tabletop: epoxy and hardwood
Epoxy Coloring Method: clear
Finish: hardwax oil

Minimalist Table
This tabletop is mostly constructed from epoxy, using just a sliver of wood to bring a natural beauty to the piece.

Dimensions: Approx. 84" x 48" (213.4 x 121.9cm)
Tabletop: epoxy and hardwood
Epoxy Coloring Method: tint dye
Leg Construction/Material: unknown
Finish: unknown

Spalted Dark Hardwood
The slabs in this table have a bit of spalting—a mold that forms in the tree while it's alive—that gives the table even more depth.

Dimensions: Approx. 144" x 44" (365.8 x 111.8cm)
Tabletop: epoxy and hardwood
Epoxy Coloring Method: dye
Leg Construction/Material: custom metal base
Finish: hardwax oil

Gallery

Ibrahim Guler | Artist and Founder of Jehoel's Work

Blue River-Style Table
This table has the traditional river-style look but is made more opulent with a custom gold-colored base.

Dimensions: Approx. 144" x 44" (365.8 x 111.8cm)
Tabletop: epoxy and hardwood
Epoxy Coloring Method: mica powder
Leg Construction/Material: custom metal bas
Finish: unknown

Dark Waters
This table uses dark black epoxy to add depth. Paired with the dark wood, this table has a classic feel that would look great in any home.

Dimensions: Approx. 144" x 44" (365.8 x 111.8cm)
Tabletop: epoxy and hardwood
Epoxy Coloring Method: dye
Leg Construction/Material: unknown
Finish: hardwax oil

Lightning Strike
This credenza uses a deep purple epoxy with arching white accents that are reminiscent of lightning in the night's sky.

Dimensions: Approx. 84" x 25" (213.4 x 63.5cm)
Tabletop: epoxy and hardwood
Epoxy Coloring Method: mica powder and dye
Finish: hardwax oil

Gallery

Ibrahim Guler | Artist and Founder of Jehoel's Work

Envy Green
This table has a semitranslucent river with just a touch of green. It's sure to make any dinner guests envious!

Dimensions: Approx. 144" x 44" (365.8 x 111.8cm)
Tabletop: epoxy and hardwood
Epoxy Coloring Method: mica powder
Leg Construction/Material: custom metal base
Finish: unknown

Industrial Table

The curly hardwood paired with the semi-translucent river is beautiful, but another eye-catcher on this table is its custom metal base that is constructed of many arching steel rods.

Dimensions: Approx. 144" x 44" (365.8 x 111.8cm)
Tabletop: epoxy and hardwood
Epoxy Coloring Method: dye
Leg Construction/Material: custom metal base
Finish: unknown

Onyx

This table uses a deep black epoxy paired with a light brown wood to create a classy, understated effect.

Dimensions: Approx. 144" x 44" (365.8 x 111.8cm)
Tabletop: epoxy and hardwood
Epoxy Coloring Method: dye
Leg Construction/Material: custom metal base
Finish: unknown

Gallery

Ibrahim Guler | Artist and Founder of Jehoel's Work®

Cast Wood
This table is mostly constructed of epoxy. The wood in the center is cast in the epoxy to give it a floating effect.

Dimensions: Approx. 54" (137.2cm) diameter
Tabletop: epoxy and hardwood
Epoxy Coloring Method: dye
Leg Construction/Material: custom metal base
Finish: unknown

Knotty Table
This table features many knots, burls, and voids, some of which are filled with black epoxy. This gives it a dynamic, layered look.

Dimensions: Approx. 84" x 48" (213.4 x 121.9cm)
Tabletop: epoxy and hardwood
Epoxy Coloring Method: dye
Leg Construction/Material: custom metal base
Finish: unknown

Placid River
The darkly colored epoxy in this river gives the impression of stillness.

Dimensions: Approx. 60" x 42" (152.4 x 106.7cm)
Tabletop: epoxy and hardwood
Epoxy Coloring Method: dye
Leg Construction/Material: steel legs
Finish: unknown

King's Table
Between it's length, it's striking blue river, and shining gold base, this table is fit for a king!

Dimensions: Approx. 144" x 44" (365.8 x 111.8cm)
Tabletop: epoxy and hardwood
Epoxy Coloring Method: mica powder
Leg Construction/Material: custom metal base
Finish: hardwax oil

Churning End Table
This small end table features a beautiful blue with white dye swirled in, giving the impression of churning waters.

Dimensions: Approx. 42" x 42" (106.7 x 106.7cm)
Tabletop: epoxy
Epoxy Coloring Method: dye, mica powder, natural materials
Leg Construction/Material: U-style metal base
Finish: hardwax oil

Ibrahim Guler | Artist and Founder of Jehoel's Work

Dining Table with Silver Base
This table features an understated silver base that can blend in well in any home.

Dimensions: Approx. 144" x 44" (365.8 x 111.8cm)
Tabletop: epoxy and hardwood
Epoxy Coloring Method: dye
Leg Construction/Material: custom metal base
Finish: hardwax oil

Kyle & Ali Johnson | Backwoods Timber Creations
Ontario, Canada

Throughout high school, Kyle worked at Keeso's Sawmill in Listowel, where his passion for woodworking truly began. After he graduated, he began working at Bauman Sawmill in Wallenstein and was introduced to live edge wood. He began experimenting with it by making furniture pieces on the side for friends and family, and it wasn't too long that word started to get out about his beautiful creations. In the spring of 2015, he decided to take the leap and start working with live edge furniture full time, and Backwoods Timber Creations was born! A few years later, Ali jumped on board full time to run the storefront and handle all marketing, communication, and administrative duties, giving Kyle more time to focus on making furniture.

Spalted Maple Table
This table features spalted maple wood with epoxy accents and a black base.

Dimensions: Approx. 24" x 42" (61 x 106.7cm)
Tabletop: epoxy and spalted maple
Epoxy Coloring Method: dye
Leg Construction/Material: U-style metal base
Finish: hardwax oil

Kyle & Ali Johnson | Backwoods Timber Creations

Swirling River
In addition to the beautiful figuring in this hardwood, this swirling river effect—achieved by introducing small amounts of white dye into the blue epoxy—is sure to be an eye-catcher.

Dimensions: 35" (89cm) diameter
Tabletop: epoxy and hardwood
Epoxy Coloring Method: mica powder
Leg Construction/Material: unknown
Finish: hardwax oil

Tundra Table
The maple burls in this icy blue epoxy create a chilling and beautiful effect.

Dimensions: Approx. 34" x 42" (86.4 x 106.7cm)
Tabletop: epoxy and maple burl
Epoxy Coloring Method: mica powder
Leg Construction/Material: custom metal base
Finish: hardwax oil

Maple Burl Coffee Table
This coffee table features maple burls cast in black epoxy. The burls almost look like leaves floating on dark water!

Dimensions: 34" x 36" (86.4 x 91.4cm)
Tabletop: epoxy and maple burl
Epoxy Coloring Method: dye
Leg Construction/Material: custom metal base
Finish: hardwax oil

Walnut Coffee Table
This table features a walnut slab cast in blue-gray, swirling epoxy.

Dimensions: 35" (89cm) diameter
Tabletop: epoxy and walnut
Epoxy Coloring Method: mica powder
Leg Construction/Material: walnut base
Finish: hardwax oil

Lindsay Russell | Backwood Design Co.
Ontario, Canada

I source and hand-select only unique, sustainably harvested lumber to design and create each of my pieces. Using color theory, interior design influence, and inspiration from nature, I love to design and create one-of-a-kind conversational pieces for your home and business. Most of my inspiration comes from the area where I live. I am surrounded by hardwood forests and the rocky, granite shorelines of the Georgian Bay. The area flaunts an incredible palette of earthy tones, brilliant blues, and an incredible display of colors in the fall. It's stunning, and I always to try to bring that same vibe into the home. I also enjoy inspiring others to find their own style and creativity when it comes to woodworking and epoxy art, and have had the honor of teaching thousands of artists, woodworkers, and students worldwide how to work with epoxy.

Black Walnut Set
This black walnut dining and coffee table set were for a wonderful couple in Muskoka! They wanted a river-style epoxy table, but wanted it to appear to be thick glass. I used a transparent black pigment to create a translucent black color so the light could slightly pass through. I sanded to a high grit and then used polishing compounds to achieve the glass-like reflection on the epoxy. Both bases were custom designed, fabricated, and then powder-coated in satin black for a durable paint finish.

Dimensions: 30" x 48" (76.2 x 121.9cm)
Tabletop: black walnut
Epoxy Coloring Method: resin pigment
Leg Construction/Material: steel base
Finish: hardwax oil

Dimensions: 60" (152.4cm) diameter
Tabletop: black walnut
Epoxy Coloring Method: resin pigment
Leg Construction/Material: steel base
Finish: hardwax oil

Lindsay Russell | Backwood Design Co.

Peninsula Table
This was such a fun project to work on and try a new technique! This client had a very specific idea in mind, and together we brought this piece to life. They wanted a very natural river-style look and they wanted the rivers to look like soapstone to match their countertops. This was a technique that I had never tried before, and although it was challenging, the voids look so similar to their countertops. The client was thrilled with the final outcome, and I learned something new in the process.

Dimensions: 60" x 36" (152.4 x 91.4cm)
Tabletop: black walnut and epoxy
Epoxy Coloring Method: mica powder and epoxy pigments
Leg Construction/Material: black walnut leg on one end and joined at a counter on the other
Finish: hardwax oil

Round Walnut Table
This table was a challenge to pour at the time. Epoxy compositions and chemicals have changed and evolved over the years to be able to handle large volumes being poured at once. When this piece was made, those weren't available on the market yet. This was over 60 liters of epoxy poured into a mold at one time. We were really pushing and testing the limits of the epoxy on this piece.

Dimensions: 50" (127cm) diameter
Tabletop: wormy ash and epoxy
Epoxy Coloring Method: white mica powder and white liquid epoxy pigments
Leg Construction/Material: red oak
Finish: hardwax oil

Sugar Maple Table
This client loved the look of a traditional river-style table, but she wanted it to be more subtle and natural. For this coffee table, I opted for a smaller, interesting crotch piece where the main trunk split off with a smaller branch. This slab also had some very deep and interesting bark inclusions, so I added a highlight layer of turquoise mica powder before filling the voids with clear. In the main void, I did multiple, thinner layers of epoxy and used my ocean technique to create waves for a natural water effect. Once that cured, the remainder of the void was filled with clear epoxy to level off the top surface of the table.

Dimensions: 48" x 36" (121.9 x 91.4cm)
Tabletop: figured sugar maple and epoxy
Epoxy Coloring Method: mica powder with liquid pigment
Leg Construction/Material: steel base
Finish: hardwax oil

Gallery

Nick DeMao | WoodEyes Woodworks
Georgia, United States

I've been in business for a little over eight years and specialize in handcrafted furniture of all shapes and sizes. I began by making small gifts such as bottle openers and beer caddies, but over time have carved out a niche building bespoke furniture. Every piece is handled solely by me from start to finish.

Hunter Green Table
This is a close-up of an iridescent spalted maple river-style table that boasted a hunter green epoxy. In direct sunlight, the epoxy shines beautifully to create this gorgeous effect.

Dimensions: 36" x 60" (91.4 x 152.4cm)
Tabletop: spalted maple
Epoxy Coloring Method: mica powder
Finish: hardwax oil

Spalted Maple Table

I used spalted maple slabs for this table, along with epoxy blended with two types of green mica pigments. The legs are constructed of heavy duty steel tubes that have been powder-coated black.

Dimensions: 36" x 96" (91.4 x 243.8cm)
Tabletop: spalted maple
Epoxy Coloring Method: mica powder
Leg Construction/Material: steel tube
Finish: natural oil

Nick DeMao | WoodEyes Woodworks

Pecky Table
For this table, I used pecky cypress salvaged from barns in Louisiana. I handcrafted the legs out of solid cypress.

Dimensions: 24" x 48" (61 x 121.9cm)
Tabletop: pecky cypress
Epoxy Coloring Method: liquid resin pigment
Leg Construction/Material: cypress
Finish: varnish

English Elm
I used English elm for the tabletop, along with an epoxy mixed with a blue metallic pigment.

Dimensions: 36" x 60" (91.4 x 152.4cm)
Tabletop: English elm
Epoxy Coloring Method: liquid resin pigment
Leg Construction/Material: steel
Finish: natural oil

Nick Hunter | Hunter Edge Woodworks
Ontario, Canada

My family runs a sawmill in Gooderham, Ontario, called M.W. Hunter Lumber, and I work for them as the main sawyer. I began my woodworking journey in 2018 after watching some YouTube videos of wood and epoxy tables being made. It was amazing, and I didn't think anything could be cooler. It became my goal to make an amazing river-style table, so I did. After the first table was done, I was excited for the potential for this to be my new career. Three years and 100+ projects later, I'm still building and experimenting with functional art, chasing the dream of full-time business.

Blue Streak
This table features a blue epoxy streak, colored with mica powder. The wood is spalted maple. This is a great beginner project.

Dimensions: 20" x 36" (50.8 x 91.4cm)
Tabletop: spalted maple
Epoxy Coloring Method: mica powder
Leg Construction/Material: Z-style base
Finish: hardwax oil

Nick Hunter | Hunter Edge Woodworks

Walnut End Table
This table features black walnut cast in a clear epoxy. The base is custom made from a salvaged chain that has been welded to provide rigidity.

Dimensions: 20" x 20" (50.8 x 50.8cm)
Tabletop: black walnut
Epoxy Coloring Method: clear epoxy cast
Leg Construction/Material: salvaged chain-link base
Finish: high gloss tabletop epoxy

Game On
This is a custom gaming desk made with black walnut. The epoxy is clear, and LED lights are set into the table to provide a red glow.

Dimensions: 20" x 40" (50.8 x 101.6cm)
Tabletop: black walnut
Epoxy Coloring Method: mica powder
Leg Construction/Material: steel
Finish: hardwax oil

Small Coffee Table
This coffee table is made with a black walnut veneer, which is a really inexpensive way to incorporate wood into an epoxy table. The epoxy is solid black with a matte finish.

Dimensions: 20" x 40" (50.8 x 101.6cm)
Tabletop: black walnut
Epoxy Coloring Method: dye
Leg Construction/Material: custom steel base
Finish: hardwax oil

Black Walnut Dining Table
This dining table features black walnut slabs and a semitransparent blue epoxy river.

Dimensions: 36" x 64" (91.4 x 162.6cm)
Tabletop: black walnut
Epoxy Coloring Method: mica powder
Leg Construction/Material: hourglass steel base
Finish: high gloss tabletop epoxy

Nick Hunter | Hunter Edge Woodworks

Galaxy Table
This table uses black walnut slabs. The epoxy river has a galaxy effect achieved by using black dye and various glitters.

Dimensions: 28" x 60" (71.1 x 152.4cm)
Tabletop: black walnut
Epoxy Coloring Method: dye and glitter
Leg Construction/Material: hourglass steel base
Finish: high gloss tabletop epoxy

Spalted Maple Coffee Table
This coffee table uses spalted maple slabs. The dark lines created by the spalting pair well with the black epoxy river.

Dimensions: 24" x 24" (61 x 61cm)
Tabletop: spalted maple
Epoxy Coloring Method: mica powder
Leg Construction/Material: L-style steel base
Finish: high gloss tabletop epoxy

Rachel Walker-Hook | Chessie Goes Wild ART
Oregon, United States

Starting from the base steps of flattening and sanding the wood, to the underpainting and layering of the epoxy resin, I pour my soul into my work. It's not about making a product. It's about making something truly special for each client. My art has given me freedom in being able to express the unexpressable traumas of my past and move forward with hope for the future.

Ocean Table
This table was commissioned during the height of the COVID-19 pandemic. And as more commissions rolled in, I soon realized that my tables were operating as more than just a surface. They were bringing peace and hope to people's homes, as they dreamt of seeing the ocean in person again. With that in mind, creating these tables became more than making an object. With every stroke of paint or pigment I mix, I put my whole heart into it. I paint in details at every layer instead of just using epoxy effects, and layer epoxy up to 10 times to achieve the right 3D look on the wood. With the standard being 1–3 layers, some may call it excessive—but I think that's exactly what you need at times to be extraordinary.

Dimensions: 48" x 23" (121.9 x 58.4cm)
Tabletop: spalted maple
Epoxy Coloring Method: mica powder, oxide pigments, transparent pigments, and acrylic ink
Leg Construction/Material: U-style steel base
Finish: resin

Tools and Materials

The goal of this book is to make river-style table construction an approachable endeavor for any beginning carpenter. While this tools list may seem extensive, all the required tools can be purchased for an initial startup cost of around $500–$700. With that in mind, here are the tools you will need to complete these projects:

TOOLS

Circular saw—A circular saw is a power tool that cuts materials using a circular blade. There are many quality circular saws available for purchase, and the one you should select just depends on the budget of your shop. I recommend a track saw, no matter the brand you go with. Simply put, a track saw is a circular saw that is attached to a track that makes for more accurate cuts. This handheld saw makes 100 percent straight cuts that do not need jointer work for gluing. If this is not an option for you, a high-quality brand circular saw will work, so long as it is paired with a straight edge for a guide.

Orbital sander—Orbital sanders are handheld power tools that work by rotating themselves elliptically. When sandpaper is attached, this rotation allows you to smooth out surfaces quickly. The orbital sander I use is electric with a hook-and-loop pad. This also has a vacuum hookup that sucks dust through the sander's pad and helps a lot with keeping the dust level to a minimum. A pneumatic sander is excellent, as well, but generally does not have a dust vacuum setup and requires an air compressor for use.

Handheld belt sander—A handheld belt sander is a powered tool that uses belts with an abrasive coating (basically sandpaper) to quickly remove material. These are particularly effective for working with wood. I recommend a belt sander with a 4" (10cm) belt (which is more than wide enough for the projects we'll be doing). This helps keep the sander steady and prevents it rocking from side to side.

Sandpaper—There is no one type of sandpaper to use. I recommend using sandpaper with a cloth or net backing. Paper-backed sandpaper rips easily, and for applications such as live edge work, does not last long and can risk damage to your sander pad.

Square—A quality square is a must. This will be used to make the end of your table a perfect 45-degree angle and is useful for most projects in a woodshop.

Tape measure—This will be used in almost every stage of the building process.

Pencil/marker—For marking measurements, cut lines, etc.

Straight edge—You can use a straight board or any other material with a straight edge you can follow to make straight marks and cuts.

Caulking gun/caulk—A caulking gun is used to apply caulk to a surface. Caulk is used as an adhesive sealant.

Sheathing tape (two rolls)—We will use sheathing tape to create an epoxy-proof barrier on our river-style table form.

Drill—Most cordless drills will work for this project. I recommend a 12- or 18-volt powered drill with a ½" (13mm) chuck (the cylindrical clamp that holds your drill bit in place).

Drill bits—For precision woodworking, I recommend high-speed steel drill bits with brad point tip. This is so the drill bit does not wander when starting a hole. We will use the following bit sizes: 1" (2.54cm), ¼" (6.4mm), ⅜" (1cm), and ⁵⁄₁₆" (7.9mm). We will also use ³⁄₁₆" (4.8mm) and ⅜" (10mm) countersink drill bits. A countersink bit is used to create an area in the wood that matches the countersunk shape of a screw/bolt head.

Drilling jig—In Chapter 7, I will detail the process for creating a drilling jig. This custom tool will help us join our tabletops to our table legs by showing us precisely where to drill our holes for dowels or screws/bolts.

Straight screwdriver—This will be used for removing bark in places you cannot reach with your chisel.

Hammer—I use two types of hammers. The main one is a mallet with rubber and plastic at either end. The other is a small metal hammer for light work because the smaller size makes it easier to use.

Chisel—For this project, I mainly use two sizes of chisels: ½" and 1" (12 and 25mm). A regular wood chisel with a straight edge is excellent. Don't use a thin chisel, as that is designed for fine woodcarving.

Rotary tool—A rotary tool is a handheld power tool that is mainly used for grinding, sanding, and polishing a variety of materials.

Rotary burr—Also known as a carbide burr, a rotary burr is a small drill or rotary tool attachment that is used for cutting, shaping, and grinding a variety of materials. For general use and for what we will be using them for in this book, a rotary burr with a ¼" (6mm) shaft and round nose shape is perfect.

Wire wheel brush—Wire wheel brushes come in many forms, but the most common are those made as attachments for drills, bench grinders, or angle grinders. They have wires made of metal that are great for scraping away unwanted material (such as bark). A wire wheel with a medium-coarse wire that is designed to be used with hand drills is what I will be using.

Abrasive wheel—An abrasive wheel is made of small, abrasive particles and is used for grinding away unwanted material. These are most commonly used with drills, rotary tools, bench grinders, and angle grinders. I will be using an abrasive wheel with 80-grit abrasive.

Power planer—In simplest terms, a power planer is a machine used to make the surfaces of boards even and flat, though we will discuss the differences between planed and flattened wood later in this book. Almost any power planer will work. As long as it is a quality brand, you should be fine!

POWER PLANER

Router—A router is a power tool used to hollow out (rout) areas in materials such as wood. It has many uses, but we will be using it primarily to smooth the edges of our wood. A small trim router is excellent for this type of project, as they are small and easy to handle. Cordless routers are handy but not a necessity.

Router bits—I will be using a ⅛" (3mm) roundover bit. Many brands make them, but make sure it is a carbide tip. As long as it is from a quality brand, you should be able to rout with it for years!

ROUTER

Clamps—Clamps are used to temporarily hold your wood together during processes like glue-up. The size you will need will depend upon the project's size. A safe bet is to get clamps that are 36" (91.4cm) long. They can always be adjusted for smaller workpieces, but you cannot make clamps larger. The best types of clamps for what we will be doing are F-clamps. These have wide jaws and can be adjusted to various widths. If using a prebuilt form for your river-style table, you will also need large C-clamps.

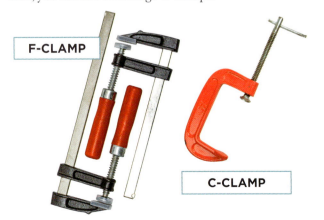

F-CLAMP

C-CLAMP

Spokeshave—There are many types of spokeshaves and each spokeshave can be used for a multitude of tasks. In some ways, it is like a planer in that it is used to smooth wood surfaces. We will be using this tool to help remove bark, so a normal spokeshave is fine. I prefer the style with a curved blade.

SPOKESHAVE

Mixing stick or drill paint mixer—You will need either a mixing stick or a drill paint mixer—a drill attachment—to mix your epoxy.

Mixing container—You will need a container (such as a bucket) in which to mix your epoxy.

Fan—A common box fan will do. This will be used for helping epoxy cure on your river-style table.

BOX FAN

Propane torch—There are many propane torches available, and most will suit our purposes, though I advise getting one with at least a 14-oz. tank. We will use this to pop bubbles in our epoxy and in some finishing techniques.

Hairdryer—Any hairdryer will work for our purposes. This will be used in creating our tables with the ocean effect.

PROPANE TORCH

HAIR DRYER

CA glue and activator—While not a "tool" in the most traditional sense, I am including these items in our list because many might not be familiar with them. CA glue is most commonly known as superglue. In addition to being an adhesive, this glue is terrific for filling gaps and voids in wood. CA glue activator is a solvent that can be sprayed on CA glue to speed up the drying process.

Small brush—We will use this for spreading small amounts of epoxy.

Building Wood and Resin River-Style Tables

Super polish scrubbing pads—This is a pad made of polyester fibers that we will use to apply oil to our finished tables and buff them.

Small syringe—This can be helpful in spreading dyed epoxy for our tables with the ocean effect, though you can also use a small stick.

SMALL SYRINGE

Dust collector—I use a variety of machines for dust collection. What you should use varies a lot by your space and your budget. The main machine I use is a stand-alone outdoor dust collector that has pipes running throughout the shop. This is not something most people will have in a small shop or garage, nor is it necessary for anyone outside of professionals. For beginners and small applications, I recommend a portable dust collector along with a shop vac. These can be purchased online or from any home improvement store.

MATERIALS

The prices of materials are always fluctuating, but to get quality materials for a river-style table, you can expect to shell out between $800—$1,600 to create something the size of an average dining room table and between $150–$400 for a small coffee table or end table.

Melamine or plywood—We can use either of these materials for constructing our river-style table form. Melamine is often cheaper than plywood, but it is denser, which can make it more difficult to work. You should get melamine or plywood that is ¾"–1" (1.9–2.5cm) thick. Exact width and length will vary depending upon the table you are making. Your length and width of your melamine/plywood should each measure 3" (7.6cm) more than you want your finished table to be.

Prebuilt form (optional)— I will use a prebuilt form for our rocky river coffee table. The dimensions for this form are 24" x 48" (61 x 122cm) at the bottom and 25" x 49" (63.5 x 124.5cm) at the top. You can also build a form to these dimensions. If you do not wish to build a form for your own custom table size, you can purchase a prebuilt one from any major home improvement store.

SCREWS

Screws—These will be used for building your river-style table form and your drilling jig. You will need 1½" (3.8cm) screws and 3" (7.6cm) screws.

Boards—You will need a variety of boards to complete the projects in this book. The sizes of the boards you will need are specific to the project, so please check the materials section of each project you are undertaking for precise measurements.

Casting epoxy—Casting epoxy is used for creating molds, forms, and other applications. This will be used to make your table.

Tabletop epoxy—Tabletop epoxy is traditionally used for an epoxy finish. We will also use it to fill small holes and voids in your table.

CASTING EPOXY

Color additive—This will be used to give your epoxy color. There are three main types of color additive to use in epoxy: metallic pigment/mica powder, dye, and tint dye. We will discuss the differences in Chapter 5 of this book.

Stones/shells/other objects—If you choose to make a rocky river coffee table, you will need these to embed in your table's river.

Wood scraps—You never know what you might need some extra wood scraps for. In this case, though, they will be helpful for removing your tabletop from its form.

SHELLS AND ROCKS

Dowels/pegs—These will be used to join your tabletop to your legs. We will be using 1½" and 2" (3.8 and 5.1cm) dowels. The number you need will depend on the size of your table, but they are cheap and small, so I recommend having a few dozen on hand.

Wood glue—Wood glue is used to bond pieces of wood together.

Bolts—Sizes will vary based upon the needs of your table you will need screws or bolts to attach your table legs to your table.

Finishing oil—This will make the wood grain in your table really pop, as well as protect it from moisture. I recommend natural finishing oils such as linseed oil or tung oil.

Gloves—Use thick gloves when carrying/moving wood. When working with epoxy or finishing oils, it is recommended to wear rubber gloves of some type, as epoxy and oil finishes are hard to wash off.

WORK GLOVES

Towels—For buffing your table.

SAFETY

Please Keep the Following Safety Measures in Mind

Be sure to wear the required safety equipment, especially when dealing with epoxy. Epoxy is safe to use indoors but there are precautions to take.

- Wear gloves.
- Make sure your work area is well ventilated.
- Wear safety goggles (especially when pouring, as splashes could fly toward your face).
- Wear a respirator anytime you are working with epoxy. Not all brands will recommend this, but it's the safest practice, as epoxy can be extremely harmful to your lungs—especially when sanding.

When working with wood be sure to use adequate safety precautions.

- Use a dust collection system.
- Wear a mask or respirator.
- Wear safety glasses when working with hand tools and power tools, which could result in flying debris.
- Do not wear safety gloves when working with power tools, as gloves can get snagged by powered equipment.
- Wear proper clothing and footwear when working with moving power tools and heavy wood slabs. Loose fabrics can create safety hazards due to the possibility of snagging on powered tools. You should always wear close-toed shoes when working in a shop. When moving heavy objects, such as the wood slabs, steel-toed boots are the best footwear, as they will minimize the possibility of injury if a heavy object is dropped on your foot.

CHAPTER 1:
Introduction to Live Edge Furniture

Are you looking to build a one-of-a-kind table? In this book, I will walk you through the process of building your own river-style table. They are as one of a kind as you can get. No two tables will be alike, and each will have its own unique character. But first, let us look at the history of live edge furniture and how it came to be.

Live edge products have existed as long as people have been making wooden furniture. It is a very straightforward way to build furniture, especially tables. A live edge slab of wood is one that does not have finished edges. This means it retains the natural shape of the tree and often still has bark attached. In "the old days," it was not as simple as grabbing your cordless circular saw and cutting off the live edge. You would have had to get your handsaw and spend time cutting off the outer portion of the wood. Instead, they left the natural edge on—not as a style choice, but for convenience's sake. Once it became easier and easier to remove the natural lining from wood, the live edge fell out of fashion. While this natural look has recently become popular, this is not the start of the story. Back in 1946, George Nakashima, an award-winning architect and designer, brought live edge designs to life in his collections. Soon after, they began appearing in modern homes and have increased in popularity ever since. The past decade has seen a significant increase in live edge products, with big-name interior designers and architects offering clients stunning live edge furniture options. You can find live edge furniture in restaurants, offices, conference rooms, kitchens, and most places where you can put a table.

George Nakashima popularized live edge slabs with his furniture designs.

Greg Klassen–style River Tables use glass instead of epoxy.

This history of river-style tables is not very long. These creations are a new design style that has become more popular in the last decade. This design takes the more rustic furniture style of live edge and turns it into modern, functional furniture. Greg Klassen is the man who created the river-style table. He started coming up with furniture designs in his garage, hardly making ends meet. After coming up with the river-style table design, it was not until he went to four shows that he was able to sell it. Now, he has a steady back order on his tables that keeps him very busy! Instead of using epoxy for the river, his design uses a sheet of glass inset into the wood that bridges the space between the live edges. Over time, this style grew and became popular. Most river-style tables made currently use epoxy resin in place of the glass initially used by Greg. The technique I will teach you will use epoxy and is much more user-friendly.

In this book, I will show you three different styles of tables. First, we'll look at a dining room table with a waterfall leg. A waterfall leg is made from the same slab and epoxy and joined at a 90-degree angle, causing the character and grain of the wood to "flow" from the tabletop, around the end of the table, and down to the floor. You can apply the steps used in making this table to almost any style of table or a multitude of other projects (cutting boards, kitchen counters, credenzas, etc.).

The last tabletop we will make is an end table. On this, we will create an ocean effect. This is an excellent project for those of you that like a bit of an artistic and personal touch to your pieces. We will make wooden legs for this table using the Shou Sugi Ban finishing method, a Japanese technique from the 18th century.

A waterfall-style table utilizes the same slab of wood to create a leg and tabletop.

The next is a coffee table with embedded objects. I will be using stones, but you can encase anything in the epoxy—seashells, crystals, nuts and bolts, or anything memorable to you that you would like held in a piece of furniture for years to come! This can be done on any table and is just as simple as laying your items in the empty "river" before you pour it. Purchasing metal table legs from an artisan vendor is another option we will explore with this table.

Tables with resin can be left plain or decorated with encased seashells.

Tables with an ocean effect bring two natural styles together.

The methods I use to make the forms and other techniques are not the only way this can be done. I have found they are an easy way to step out and try your hand at river-style tables, but also work great if you want to make tables as more than just a hobby.

CHAPTER 2:
Selecting Live Edge Slabs

Keys for Selecting Live Edge Slabs
- Only get kiln-dried wood
- Use hardwood
- Buy slabs that have been planed and flattened

Live edge slab suppliers have a vast selection of woods to choose from.

Selecting the live edge slabs you want to use for your table is probably the most crucial step in making your new furniture piece. There are many things to consider during this step, but the wood is the foundation of the table, so you must start with great wood to end up with a great table!

First, and most importantly, you will need kiln-dried wood. Kiln-dried wood is critical in ensuring that your table does not warp or twist over time. The slabs you are looking for will need to be air- and kiln-dried—getting both is not as easy as you'd expect. When talking to a slab seller, they may say, "Yes, these slabs are dried. They have been cut and air-drying for six years." This may sound like the slabs have been drying long enough, but let me explain what kiln-drying wood does versus air-drying it. Kiln-drying takes the wood to a lower moisture percentage than air-drying can. This process closes the wood cells so that moisture cannot rise and fall in the slabs. If this were to happen, the slab would start to warp and twist. Your once-perfect and straight table will no longer sit level, and worse, could develop cracks or separate from the epoxy river. Another benefit of kiln-drying is that bugs that had made the tree their home could still live a good life in voids or holes in your slab, even after the slabs are cut out of the tree. When the slab goes through the kiln-drying process, the heat will kill any critters that may have been in your slab. This will eliminate the bugs from being a problem when you are pouring epoxy into your table or when that piece of furniture is in your home.

Now that you know what to look for in terms of how the slabs have been prepared, the next thing to consider is which wood type you want to use. It is best to stick with hardwoods, as they have tighter grain structures that help prevent warping due to moisture in the wood's pores. Stay away from softwoods like pine, cottonwood, fir, etc. Instead, go with a hardwood such as some type of walnut, maple, cherry, oak, or any other of the many hardwoods available from your preferred supplier.

When picking out a live edge slab, the shape is one of the main things that will determine your finished table's look and style. You will want your final product to have an excellent flowing river design, so you will need to select wood slabs with a shape to accommodate that. On the river-style tables I make, I do not cut the inside live edge. Because of this, you must select a slab that naturally gives the design you have in mind. Doing this takes time. You'll need to either browse online through many pictures from sellers that can ship to you or go to a few nearby live edge suppliers and look at their available slabs.

Non-Ideal Shape

Ideal Shape

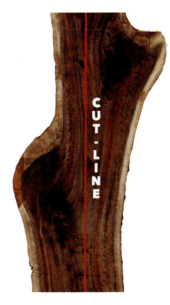

An ideal shape for your live edge slab is one that will lend itself well to mimicking the natural bends of a river. As we will cut down the center of the wood, try to visualize the slab cut in two, with the outside live edges turned inward.

When selecting your slabs, make sure the live edges of the slab are nice, solid wood and are not funky or rotten. If there is bark on the edges, that is fine, but the bark will need to be removed when you prepare the slabs for pouring epoxy. This topic will be explored in Chapter 3.

The thickness of the slabs is essential, as well. Generally, these tables look best when they are in the 1¾"–2½" (4.4–6.4cm) range of thickness, so it is best to get a slab within that thickness range rather than settling on a thinner slab. But remember, the thicker the slab, the more epoxy you will need to pour.

When selecting slabs, check for any warping that may have occurred during the drying process. For this reason, I buy slabs that have been planed or flattened. There is a critical difference between planed and flattened slabs. Flattened means precisely what it sounds like: the slabs are flat. Buying a flattened slab gives you something solid to start with, which can be finished up with hand tools. Otherwise, you need to build a flattening planer to make just one or two tables or search to find a commercial shop to rent a planer for an hour. This will save you hours of work and frustration when you are pouring epoxy and sanding your table. Planed means the slab was run through a planer. This does not mean it is flat. This only makes the slab's surface smooth and removes the rough saw cut. Many suppliers offer their slabs pre-planed; if not, most offer that service for an additional fee. If the slab is warped, running it through a planer does not necessarily remove much warp. Because of this, I always recommend contacting the slab seller and having them look or going there yourself to confirm if the planed slabs are entirely flat. If they are warped, slabs have the tendency to rock around!

Determining if your slab is warped is very important because warped slabs can be hard to seal to a form. This is because they do not lay flush against it. Like all liquids, epoxy will spread out evenly over the surface upon which it is poured. If your surface is not level, your epoxy will not be either, which will create an uneven tabletop once it has cured. So, a warped slab could have edges that you will need to plane off.

If you are not able to source slabs from a local supplier, online suppliers will ship them right to your door.

Rough Cut Not Planed/Flattened

Planed/Flattened

The slab on the left is rough cut, meaning it has not yet been planed/flattened. The slab on the right has been planed/flattened.

76   Building Wood and Resin River-Style Tables

CHAPTER 3:
Preparing Live Edge Slabs for Pouring Epoxy

Keys for Removing Bark
- No matter how tight the bark is, it must be removed for pouring an epoxy river
- A chisel and hammer are your go-to tools
- Remove as much of the cambium layer as you can
- Trim your project a few inches larger than your final size

Now that all the searching for wood is done, let's get to the fun part, building the table! It may look like a daunting task, but it is one of the easiest ways to make a one-of-a-kind table.

Tools & Materials
- Chisel
- Hammer
- Spokeshave
- Straight screwdriver
- Drill/rotary tool
- Rotary burr (optional)
- Orbital sander
- Sandpaper
- Wire wheel or abrasive wheel
- Straight edge (such as a board or piece of string)
- Circular saw or band saw
- Square
- Pencil

Before we can begin building our table, we must first prepare our slabs. In this chapter, we'll cover removing the bark and cambium layer from your slab and cutting it to size. These are some of the most crucial steps in the process of building a river-style table, but with patience and precision, you can pull it off flawlessly.

First, we need to remove the bark. This is a crucial step because the live edge side of the slab is the joint—the place where two pieces of wood meet and are joined—between the epoxy and wood. Even if the bark seems to be bonded very tightly to the wood, the bark will become loose over time. The epoxy will bond to the bark and not the solid wood if you leave the bark on. Then, when the bark starts to separate from the wood, the joint will begin to separate.

Removing bark can be the easiest step in making a river-style table—or one of the most challenging. It all depends on the tree and how tightly bonded the bark is. But, with dedication and an hour or so of work, you can always get it removed.

1. Use a chisel and hammer to remove the bark. To start removing the bark, use the chisel to work your way down the edge, placing the chisel's cutting edge on the wood and bark joint. Angle the chisel with the slope of the live edge to avoid gouging into the wood. With a hammer, slowly tap the chisel deeper into the bark until the bark starts to pop free or until inserting the chisel allows you to pry the bark away from the wood. Continue doing this down along the edge of the slab at any place possible. If you have relatively straight edges on your slab, you can also use a spokeshave to remove the bark in this step.

2. Use a straight screwdriver or rotary burr to remove bark that could not be reached with the chisel. If there are tight areas where the chisel did not fit or was not usable, clean the rest of the bark out with a straight screwdriver or rotary burr (whichever is best for your situation). If you have any bark inclusions on the surface of the wood, the rotary burr works great for that. Slowly chew away at the bark, being careful not to gouge into the wood or alter the natural flow of the grain around the inclusion.

3. Remove the cambium layer. Now that the bulk of the bark is removed, remove as much of the cambium layer as possible. The cambium cell layer is a thin, skin-like layer directly underneath the bark and against the wood. This layer is waterproof and will prevent the epoxy from seeping into and bonding to the wood. In the picture above, you can see the white section in the center where I removed a small area of the cambium. You can see the remaining cambium layer on either side of the white area.

An orbital sander, either pneumatic or electric, works great for removing the cambium layer. Use 80-grit sandpaper to sand the edge any place you can't get the sander. The cambium layer sands off easily, so this is not a very difficult task.

Use a wire wheel or abrasive wheel where the sander cannot reach. With a drill, run the wheel in the sections the sander could not hit. Now that you have all the bark and cell layer removed, it's time to split the slab down the center and trim it to size!

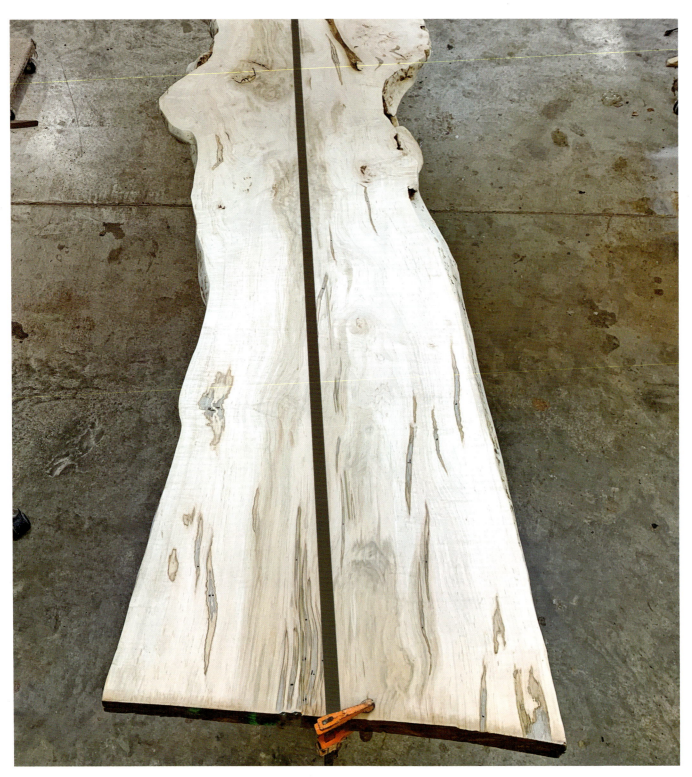

4. Use a board or piece of string to mark the cut line on your slab. To split your slab in half, there is no set dimension to go by. Where you cut it is decided by the shape and size of the slab. I recommend getting a straight board and laying it down the center to mark your cut line. You could also stretch a string down the center. This way, you can visualize where the center should be. Mark the place where you will cut.

> **TIP:** Make your table larger in length and width than needed so you can trim off any caulking right along the edges. I usually go 2" (5.1cm) longer and 1" (2.5cm) wider than the final dimensions that I want.

5. Use a circular saw to cut along your center line. Using a circular saw, make a straight cut along the line you have marked to split the table. You can use a circular saw with a track, but a simple straight-edged board will do the same thing with any circular saw. On smaller projects (such as the end table on page 99), a bandsaw will work just the same.

Chapter 3: Preparing Live Edge Slabs for Pouring Epoxy   81

6. Place the pieces of your cut slab so the live edges face the inside. Now that the slab is in two pieces, place them so the straight edges are on the outside and both live edges face each other. Move them around, slide them side to side, and move them closer and farther apart until you have created what you had envisioned from the beginning!

8. Trim the ends of your slab. With a circular saw, follow the mark you made and trim both ends. Many times, you will also have to retrim the sides depending on how you positioned the slabs to get the river shape you wanted.

7. Use a square to mark the ends where your slabs will be cut. Now that you have the slabs positioned how you want them to be poured, get a square and mark the ends where they will be trimmed. Do this by placing one arm of the square along the straight outside edge of the split slab. Using a pencil, mark each end to the approximate size you want the table to be when finished. I usually make the slabs 2" (12.7cm) longer than the length I want to end up with so I can quickly get it trimmed to the size I want. See "Finishing the Ends of the Rocky River Coffee Table" on page 83 if you are working on that project.

Finishing the Ends of the Rocky River Coffee Table

For the coffee table, the trimming of the slabs is just a bit different than it was for the dining table and end table. Since this will be poured using a prebuilt form, our slab size is determined by the size of our form, which is 24" x 48" (61 x 122cm) at the bottom and 25" x 49" (63.5 x 124.5cm) at the top. This is unlike the dining table and end table, where the form size is determined by the size we cut our slabs.

Trim both ends and sides with the saw set on an angle to match your form.

The form for the coffee table has tapered edges to make removing the poured table easier. After our slabs are split, trim them to size with the saw set at a 12-degree angle to match the slope of the form. If we were not to do this, the gap along the edges would fill with epoxy, resulting in a decent amount of epoxy that will just get cut off.

CHAPTER 4:
Making an Epoxy Table Form

Keys to Making a Form

- » A sheathing tape or plywood form is the most versatile
- » A prebuilt form cannot leak and can be reused time and time again
- » Always have caulk on hand in case the epoxy finds a gap in your form
- » More is better when putting on a caulk bead

Now we need to make a form for our table!

Tools & Materials to Build Form

- Melamine or plywood: ¾"–1" (1.9–2.5cm) x width of table plus 3" (7.6cm) x length of table plus 3" (7.6cm)
- Two rolls of sheathing tape
- Tape measure
- Marker
- Caulking gun
- Silicone-based caulk
- Drill
- Ten 1½" (3.8cm) screws
- 1"x 3"x 8"x 2'–3' (2.5 x 7.6 x 20.3 x 61–91.4cm) end boards
- Six 3" (7.6cm) screws

Tools & Materials for Prebuilt Form

- The form (whatever size best accommodates your table plans)
- Clamps (4)

The form is arguably one of the most important steps to building a river-style table. The form you build or buy will determine the final size of your table once poured. In this chapter, we will cover the steps for building forms for any type of table, as well as how to use a prebuilt form you've purchased.

Now you need to make a form so you can pour the table! Once your form is made and your slabs (and any materials you'll include if making a table with embedded objects) are positioned, the form will serve as a mold for you to pour your epoxy into. There are two ways of doing this. The first form is handmade and can be made into any size! The second form is a prebuilt form that can be bought to make building a table straightforward. Most of this chapter will cover how to build a form from scratch. If you plan to buy a prebuilt form, you can skip ahead to the next chapter.

2. Lay your slabs on your sealed plywood. Now that the majority of the form is sealed up, lay your slabs on the plywood, positioning them exactly how you want them to be poured. Check the width of your table with your tape measure to ensure the size is the same as what you laid out. Measure at multiple points for consistency across the whole table.

1. Cover your plywood or melamine with sheathing tape. To start, decide if you are using plywood or melamine; either will work great. Melamine is cheaper and denser than plywood, but plywood can be an easier material to work with. Whichever you choose, I recommend a minimum size of ¾"–1" (1.9–2.5cm) thick x width of table plus 3" (7.6cm) x length of table plus 3" (7.6cm). If the plywood is larger than this, that is fine. This example uses a sheet of plywood. Cover your plywood with sheathing tape, which is used traditionally to secure house wrap, but is the perfect non-stick material for epoxy, laying strips of tape longways on the plywood overlapping approximately ½" (1.3cm). This will create an epoxy-proof base that we can safely pour onto. Make sure to rub the tape where it overlaps to create a secure seal.

3. Mark the corners of your slabs on the plywood. Once you have measured, double-checked, and measured again, mark all four corners with a marker. When you place the slabs back on the board, this will show you precisely where to put them.

4. Use caulk to create a barrier on your slabs. Now, flip both slabs upside down on the plywood. As a reminder, the live edge will be the interior of the table while the straight edge is the outside; this image shows the reverse. With your caulk and caulking gun, lay a bead of caulk down several inches from the live edge and run it down the length of the slab. Move toward the straight-cut edge if there are any significant holes or cracks you want to fill with epoxy. Everything from your caulking bead to the straight edge will not be sealed, and everything from your caulking bead to the live edge will be sealed up. Don't move slabs after they have been laid down against the form, or you will break your caulking barrier.

5. With a helper, position your slabs on the marks you made on your plywood. For this next step, you will need a helper. Moving one slab at a time, flip the wood so the caulk side is down. Place the corners of the slab in the corresponding markings you made on the form and slowly lay it down. Be as precise as possible so you do not shift or damage the caulk barrier you have created. Then do the same to the opposite side.

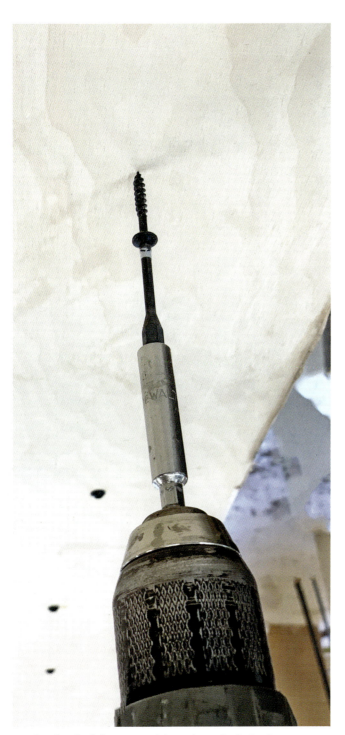

6. After both slabs are positioned precisely in the correct spots, carefully move the plywood with the slabs on top in a way that you can access half of the underside. Using a drill, fasten 1½" (3.8cm) screws through the plywood and into your slab. Start by attaching a screw in each end to hold the slab in place. Then, go down the plywood, fastening a screw every 8"–10" (20–25cm) until you reach the other end. If you need to, move the plywood so the other half is accessible from underneath, making sure it is stable. Then, repeat the process, fastening the other slab to the plywood.

7. Cut boards for sealing the edges of your form. Now you need to seal up the ends of your form. Cut a 1" x 3" (2.5 x 7.6cm) board in two. The sizes for each end board are dictated by where your caulking beads come out on either end of your table. If the measurement from one bead to the other is 11" (27.9cm), you need a board with a length of around 13" (33cm) or more. Once you know the two sizes, you need to cut the boards to length.

Chapter 4: Making an Epoxy Table Form

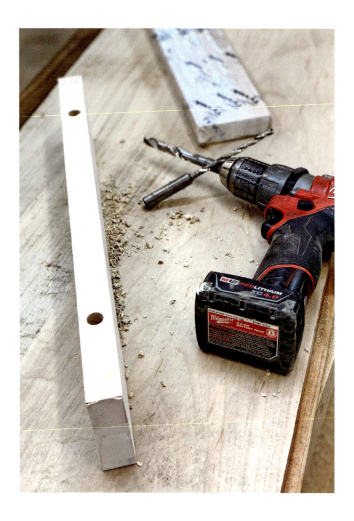

8. Drill three pilot holes per board that will be used to seal the edges of your form. Arrange the boards so the 1" (2.5cm) ends are facing up. Using a ½" (13mm) bit, drill into each board. Drill the hole approximately ½" (1.3cm) deep. Now with a ¼" (6.4mm) bit, finish drilling the hole the rest of the way through the board. Do this at each end of each board and in the boards' centers.

9. Seal your boards with sheathing tape. With sheathing tape, tape one side of each end board up 3" (7.6cm) high, overlapping it just like you did on the plywood. Make sure the side you tape is completely flat and does not have any warping.

10. Use caulk to create a barrier on the edges of your slabs. With the caulking gun, run a bead from where the caulk comes out underneath the slab straight up to the top of the slab (A to B in the image above). Do this on both slabs and at either end. Next, run a bead connecting where both caulk beads come out from underneath each slab (A to A). Do the same to the opposite end.

11. Join your end boards to the form using screws. Take one of the end boards—taped side facing your slabs and the ½" (1.3cm) holes facing up—and press it into the caulk to create a seal. Keep pressure on the slabs as you fasten your 3" (7.6cm) screws into the plywood underneath. This will hold the end board in place on the form. Your form is done! Let all the caulk dry overnight.

Coffee Table Form

For the coffee table, this step of making a form is almost nonexistent! All you need to do is pick up your slabs and set them in the form—either the one you made following the steps laid out in this chapter or a prebuilt form you've purchased. Then, grab four clamp bars or C-clamps—either will work well—and clamp the ends of both slabs so when we pour in the epoxy, the slabs do not try to float and move around. And just like that, you are done. If only all the steps were that easy!

If you are using a prebuilt form, simply set your slabs in the form and clamp them so they do not move when the epoxy is poured.

Chapter 4: Making an Epoxy Table Form

CHAPTER 5:
Preparing and Coloring Epoxy

Keys to Preparing Epoxy
- » Before you are ready to pour, you must calculate how much epoxy you will need
- » Always buy more epoxy than your calculations call for
- » There are three main ways to color your epoxy: metallic pigment, dye, and tint dye
- » Before coloring the epoxy you will use for your table, experiment with coloring epoxy on a small scale

You will soon be ready for that anticipated moment of pouring the epoxy down the river and filling it up with any color or shade that you can imagine.

Tools & Materials
- Tape measure
- Pencil
- Casting epoxy
- Tabletop epoxy
- Mixing stick or drill paint mixer
- Mixing container (such as a bucket)
- Color additive

90   Building Wood and Resin River-Style Tables

To begin, let's talk about the two types of epoxy we will be using: casting epoxy and tabletop epoxy.

Casting epoxy (right and left) and tabletop epoxy (bottom).

For pouring the river, I recommend using a casting epoxy. Different brands and types of casting epoxy will have variations on the depths that they can be poured. Some can be poured 1"–2" (2.5–5cm), and some can go up to 4"–6" (10–15cm). This measurement is how deep you can pour the epoxy at one time. If you poured a full 2" (5cm) using a 1" (2.5cm) maximum casting epoxy, it will cause problems. In this situation, the epoxy is not formulated for how you are using it. The curing process of epoxy produces heat. If you use more than directed, it could overheat and cause the epoxy river to crack or get lots of bubbles. If you use a 1" maximum pour epoxy on a 2" thick project, you must split the pouring process into two separate pours. First, you would pour 1" and let it cure (or harden). Then you would pour the final 1" and let it cure. If you are using casting epoxy formulated for 2" and up, you do the full 2" in a single pour.

Tabletop epoxy is traditionally used for an epoxy finish. For a project like this, use it to fill in small voids and cracks that you may discover after sanding your project down. If you were to use casting epoxy on a small hole to fill it up, it would not cure for up to a week or more. This is because it is such a small volume of epoxy that it would not create much heat for the curing process. Tabletop epoxy, on the other hand, should cure overnight and be ready to be worked on in the morning!

Generally, higher-cost epoxy is higher quality. Some of your cheap budget epoxies can overheat too quickly, not release bubbles, yellow, and just overall not be as good of a product. So make sure you do research on the epoxy you will be using.

Now it is time to color the epoxy, making it whatever color you want! There are three main ways you can do this:

- **Metallic pigment**—Metallic pigment, also called mica powder, is the most common coloring agent used in epoxy. This gives your epoxy the swirls and metallic ripples that you commonly see in epoxy projects. It comes in a powder form and is just a matter of adding some into the epoxy and watching the color come to life! The less mica you put in, the more translucent it is. If you want an opaque river, add more mica.

- **Dye**—Dye is often used with two primary colors: white and black. But dye can be used with other colors, as well. This gives your epoxy a solid, opaque color as if the epoxy is a substantial chunk of black or white stone perfectly fitted between two slabs of wood. If you are going for an opaque color, add the dye until you cannot see your stirring stick when it is submerged underneath the epoxy.

- **Tint dye**—You can get tint dye in any color. It is used if you want a transparent or translucent table but still want some color in the epoxy. This generally comes in a dropper bottle. Add drops until you have reached the desired color density you are looking for.

TIP: Before you add any color to the epoxy, make sure to try it on a small scale to confirm it is the color and density you want!

DYE

TINT DYE

METALLIC PIGMENT/ MICA POWDER

Here are the three most common color additives used in river-style tables.

Chapter 5: Preparing and Coloring Epoxy   91

Before pouring, you first need to figure how much epoxy you will end up using. Place a tape measure along the length of your slabs. Make a mark every 5" (12.7cm) along the river from one end to the other. Then, measure the distance from one live edge to the other at every spot you made a mark. After you have done this, add all the figures up. Next, count how many marks you made. Take your total amount of inches divided by the total number of measurements, and you will have the average width of the river.

Measure the total length of the river and the total height of your slabs. Multiply them all together. Take that number and divide it by 231 (the cubic inches in a gallon). The resulting calculation will be the approximate number of gallons of epoxy you will need to pour the table. Always buy more epoxy than this calculation calls for, since it does not take into consideration the epoxy that will seep into the edges of the wood or the small amount that will flow under the slab. If you are adding a significant number of items to your river, such as the stones in the image below, you will not need the same amount of epoxy as you would to fill the river completely. You can collect all the objects you would be using in a bucket to measure the approximate volume you would be adding. Measuring cups are also useful in a pinch. While these additions mean you will use less epoxy, it's still smart to get extra, as there will be space between the stones that will need to be filled. Now onto pouring the river!

Measure the width of the river every 5" (12.7cm) to get the average width.

CHAPTER 6:
Pouring a River-Style Table

Keys to Remember for Pouring Epoxy

- Never pour over the recommended pouring depth of your epoxy brand
- You can always pour less deep than the max depth of your epoxy brand
- Thoroughly mix epoxy; it can never be overmixed
- You can pour additional epoxy on top of casting epoxy after it has cured for 10–15 hours.
- You can pour additional epoxy on top of tabletop epoxy after it has cured for 6–8 hours.
- Always torch the epoxy after pouring to release the bubbles
- Use casting epoxy on rivers, large voids, and cracks
- Use tabletop epoxy on small voids, cracks, or river layers up to ⅛" (3mm) thick
- Let a river-style table cure for a week before removing it from the form
- Epoxy cleans up with isopropyl alcohol
- Run a fan across a river pour

Now is the exciting part! Your form is all sealed up, and your slabs are fastened down. It's time to make some decisions. What color do you want to use? How bright? Do you want to encase something in the river? The options are almost endless.

Classic River-Style Pour

Tools & Materials

- Casting epoxy
- Mixing paddle or drill paint mixer
- Mixing container (such as a bucket)
- Pigment or dye of your choice
- Propane torch
- Caulk
- Caulking gun
- Fan

Chapter 6: Pouring a River-Style Table 93

Now that you have done the math and figured out the approximate amount of epoxy you will need, it is time to get it mixed up! The casting epoxy I will be using can be poured up to 1½" (3.8cm). The slabs I am using for this waterfall table are 2" (5cm) thick, so I will do two 1" (2.5cm) pours. The casting epoxy I am using comes in a 2:1 ratio (2 parts resin to 1 part hardener). From my calculations, this table will take about six gallons total of epoxy. So, for my first pour, I will be pouring three gallons (two gallons of resin and one gallon of hardener). I like to mix the epoxy for around five to eight minutes, making sure to scrape the sides and the bottom. You want to ensure there is no unmixed epoxy. Generally, unmixed epoxy is very hazy and has swirls in it. The more you mix it, the clearer it becomes.

1. Mix your epoxy. Mix the epoxy until it is clear and there are no visible swirls of unmixed epoxy. Let the epoxy set in the container for five to ten minutes to allow some of the bubbles from mixing to rise and release from the epoxy.

2. Add color to the epoxy. Decide your color and color additive. If you are doing two pours of epoxy like I am, measure how much coloring you are putting in to do the same on the next pour. I am using a silver/pearl metallic pigment for this table. Add coloring until you have reached the perfect density of color for what you are creating.

3. Stir pigment into the epoxy. A paint mixer on a drill makes mixing the epoxy go a lot quicker, especially if it is a large amount. Check that all the coloring is mixed in and there are no clumps that have escaped your mixing.

TIP: Do not stir too fast, or you will mix a lot of bubbles in with the epoxy.

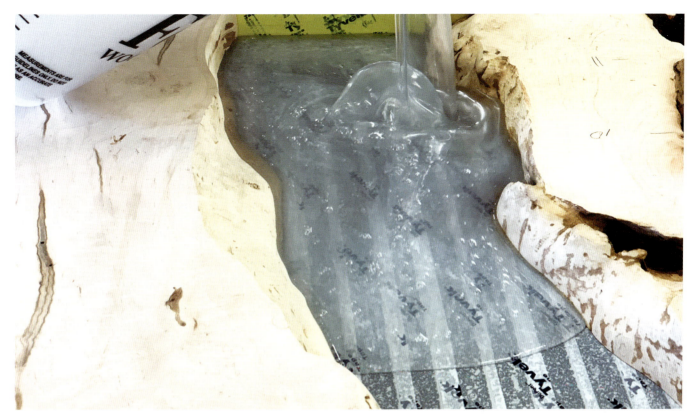

4. Pour your epoxy. It is time to pour! Slowly pour the epoxy down the open river and watch it flow down to the other end. It is best to pour from one location instead of moving around, as this will minimize the chance of messes. Do not pour it too fast or it will create a lot of extra bubbles. Pouring the epoxy onto the live edge can help reduce the bubbles, because it will gradually guide the epoxy into the form.

5. Pop bubbles in the epoxy using a propane torch. Ignite your propane torch, turn the flame down to medium/low, and go over the epoxy you just poured. This will pop the air bubbles that rise to the top and make them magically disappear. Your torch should be just a few inches from the surface of the epoxy. Do this every 15 minutes or so until there are no more bubbles coming to the surface.

6. Check for leaks in your form and let your epoxy cure. Once everything is settled, check for leaks and patch any with caulk. If your epoxy brand calls for it, place a fan so that it lightly blows across the river section as it cures. A general rule of thumb is a 1" (2.5cm) pour will not need a fan, and a 2" (5cm) or more pour should have a fan to keep the surface temperature lower. This varies by epoxy brands and how they formulate their epoxy. Some always recommend it, and some do not; if the instructions on the packaging are unclear, contact them to confirm which path you should take.

Chapter 6: Pouring a River-Style Table

7. Swirl your epoxy as needed as it cures. Several hours after the epoxy has been poured, you should check to make sure that the metallic pigment has the swirls and character you are looking for. If not, simply take a stick and slowly stir through it, making waves and patterns as you go. If the epoxy is still very runny in consistency as it was when you poured it, it is very likely the patterns will disappear as the epoxy cures. Once the epoxy becomes thicker, similar to the consistency of thick wood glue, the patterns and swirls you add should stay. Check on it every 15 minutes or so if you want a certain swirled pattern. Each time you swirl the epoxy, use the torch to pop any bubbles you created from stirring it. If the epoxy is very thick, the bubble will need the assistance of the torch to rise through the epoxy and pop.

> **TIP:** If several hours after pouring the epoxy, you have a section that is a "hard lump," but the rest is still runny, it is curing too fast. Turn the fan onto the epoxy more directly to keep it cool. Your project is fine, but you want to maintain as much air movement as possible.

> **TIP:** I recommend staying close by for at least one hour after you have poured the table, making sure there are no leaks. Always have some caulking nearby just in case. If everything is done correctly, there will not be a leak. However, if you discover a leak, do not worry. Every epoxy artisan has had a leak at some point. Caulking always stops the leaks I discover.

> **TIP:** I find that on a 1" (2.5cm) pour with a fan blowing across the table, it will generally not start becoming thick for 8–12 hours. This will vary by epoxy brand and room temperature.

8. If a second pour is needed, wait overnight or up to a day as first pour cures. The optimal time to do this is after the epoxy from your first pour has firmed up and cannot be stirred but is still tacky. It should be soft enough to press dents into it. Also, make sure it is cool to the touch. If the epoxy is firm but still warm or hot, the heat will make your final pour cure too quickly, possibly causing it to crack. Do not wait until the bottom layer is 100 percent hard when you pour your second layer. If you do, your top layer will not bond to the bottom layer of epoxy. If you have waited too long and the epoxy is totally hard, take some 220-grit sandpaper and scuff the bottom layer until it has a hazy sheen. Then, wipe off the dust from sanding and you are ready to pour again. Repeat steps 1–6, and the epoxy is done!

Rocky River Coffee Table Pour

Tools & Materials
- Objects of your choice to encase in the river
- Casting epoxy
- Black tint dye
- Mixing paddle or drill paint mixer
- Mixing container (such as a bucket)
- Propane torch

1. Place your stones in the river cavity. This process is mostly the same as detailed in pages 93–96. In this instance, however, you will be encasing rocks in the table. First, make sure the stones are free of dirt. Place them in, starting with a batch of small pebbles. Add another container of larger rocks. Finally, place a handful of larger stones. Play around with it. There is no right or wrong way! Keep the objects you are encasing an inch or two (2.5 to 5cm) away from both ends of the form. That way, you will not cut into anything when you trim the ends straight. For a natural-looking river, use many different sizes of rock.

Chapter 6: Pouring a River-Style Table

2. Combine your resin and hardener. To show off the items encased in the epoxy, keep the mixture clear or mostly translucent. I like to add just one or two drops of black tint dye for clear pours. The color will not be noticeable, but it keeps epoxy from yellowing years down the road.

3. Pour the epoxy into the river. After the epoxy is thoroughly mixed, slowly pour the epoxy into the river. When pouring, be careful that the epoxy does not move your objects around. If using an epoxy that requires two separate pours, wait until the first has hardened before pouring the second. Follow the curing instructions in steps 6–8 on pages 95 and 96 to complete this project.

Ocean End Table Pour

Tools & Materials

- Casting epoxy
- Blue metallic pigment
- White dye
- Mixing paddle or drill paint mixer
- Mixing container (such as a bucket)
- Tabletop epoxy
- Syringe, screwdriver, popsicle stick, or other stick
- Hairdryer
- Propane torch

This is the most artistic of the projects detailed in this book. You could do this on almost any table, including an end table like we are doing today!

2. Fill your river halfway with the mixed epoxy. Once you have thoroughly mixed the epoxy and the blue pigment, fill up the river section until it is around half full. Since these slabs are 2" (5cm) high, I will stop at 1" (2.5cm). Let the epoxy harden until it is firm and cool. It should still be soft enough that you can make dents by pressing on it.

1. Mix your epoxy with your chosen blue pigment and let it cure. First, figure out the amount of epoxy you will need. This time, we only want to pour to a depth of ¾"–1" (1.9–2.5cm). If you are using a 2" (5cm)-deep epoxy pour, do not pour the maximum amount. A 2" epoxy will cure at 1" thick, but it may take a day or two longer. Since this project is meant to look like an ocean, use a blue metallic pigment. The metallic swirls will give the water some depth and add some movement to the epoxy. Find a shade you like, whether it is the light blue of the Caribbean Sea, a dark blue of the deep ocean, or the blue-green of the Brazilian coast.

3. Pour a thin layer of tabletop epoxy onto your river. Now, it is time for tabletop epoxy. This is very similar to casting epoxy. The difference is that it should, on average, only be poured approximately ⅛" (3mm) thick and uses a 1:1 ratio (1 part resin to 1 part hardener). Check your specific brand's instructions before mixing and pouring. Mix a minimal amount. You want enough to put a thin, clear coat across the top of the casting epoxy you poured in the previous step. Make sure to only drizzle enough to coat the entire top of the casting epoxy, no more.

Chapter 6: Pouring a River-Style Table

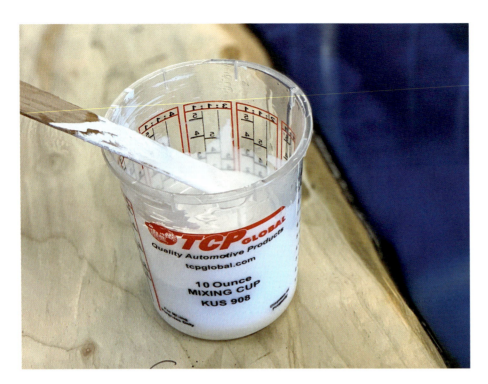

4. Mix tabletop epoxy with white dye or white acrylic paint. Now, immediately mix up approximately 2–4 fl. oz. (59–118ml) of tabletop epoxy. If you have epoxy remaining from step 3, you can use that. Next, add some white dye until it is solid white, not milky. White acrylic paint will work, as well, to turn the epoxy white.

5. Drizzle a small line of the white epoxy along the river's shoreline. The easiest way to control the application of the white dye for making waves is to get a small syringe at a local pet or art store. A popsicle stick or screwdriver will also work if used carefully. Taking your white epoxy, drizzle a small white line along the shoreline, being careful not to run it up onto the "wooden shore."

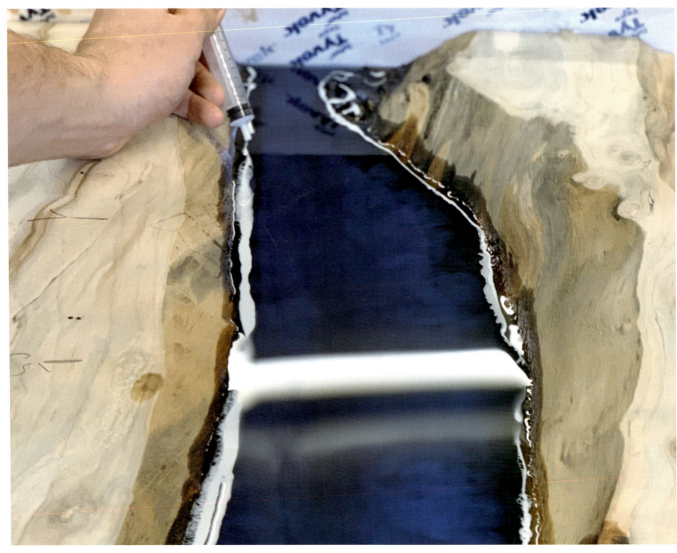

6. Use a hairdryer to spread the white epoxy out from the shoreline. You will only need this for a few minutes, so you can probably borrow this tool from a bathroom in the house. Turn the air on high and, if adjustable, turn the heat on high. Put the end close to the epoxy while pointing it away from the wood, toward the center of the river. Watch as the air blows the white streak into waves. Work your way along both live edges. If you want, blow some areas of the white waves back in the direction of the shore. Play around with this until you like the result. Check back in 10–15 minutes and make sure the waves still have the look you want. At this point, the tabletop epoxy has begun to thicken but still should be moveable with the hairdryer. Once you have touched up any areas, you are set. The epoxy will continue to thicken and fully firm up in the next few hours. Just as with casting epoxy, wait until it is firm but can still fairly easily receive dents before doing the final pour. If you want some natural wave "bubbles" in the white, use a water sprayer filled with isopropyl alcohol and spray a mist onto the white. This will make the white separate and create natural "holes" in the waves like you see at the beach.

7. Fill the rest of your river with clear casting epoxy and let cure. Mix the needed amount of clear casting epoxy. Just as you did for the rocky river table, add just a drop or two of black tint dye. Then, fill up the rest of the river with the clear casting epoxy and let it harden, popping bubbles with the torch. After the last pour on any river-style table, let it sit for a week. This will ensure the epoxy is fully cured and will not try to bend after it is removed from the form.

CHAPTER 7:
Cutting, Sanding, and Machining the Tabletop

Keys to Finishing Your Tabletop

- Do not try to remove your table from the form early
- Use epoxy to fill any small gaps or voids you find after the table has cured
- When sanding, you will likely open up small cracks and voids; fill these with CA glue
- Your waterfall table will require additional actions outside of what is needed for the other tabletops, as it will have a leg that extends from the tabletop

Now, on to finishing up your one-of-a-kind table and putting it to use!

Tools & Materials

- Sandpaper
- Tabletop epoxy
- Mixing paddle or drill paint mixer
- Mixing container (such as a bucket)
- Hammer
- Wood scraps (to use as wedges)
- Tape measure
- Hand planer
- Handheld belt sander
- Orbital sander
- CA glue and activator
- Chisel
- Circular saw/track saw
- Router
- ⅛" (3mm) roundover routing bit

Additional Tools for Waterfall Dining Table

- Two 3' (91.4cm) long boards
- Clamps (4)
- Dowels (1½" and 2" [3.8 and 5.1cm])
- Square
- Pencil
- Two 1¼" x 12" x 6" (3.2 x 30 x 15cm) boards
- ⅜" (1cm) drill bit
- 1" (25.5mm) drill bit
- Screws (size will vary depending upon need)
- Straight edge (such as a board)
- Small brush
- Wood glue
- Rubber mallet

Finishing Your Tabletop

At this point, your tabletop has cured and is ready to be taken out of the form and cut to size. In this chapter, we will cover the processes for sanding your tabletop and cutting it to size. We will also go over creating a waterfall table leg.

Once the tables have cured for a week, you are soon ready to remove them from the form. But first, there are some things to touch up, as curing the epoxy can cause dips below the tabletop's surface that should be filled.

1. Use tabletop epoxy to fill any dips, cracks, and voids in your tabletop. Take a piece of sandpaper and sand the epoxy surface you will be filling up with epoxy. Then, mix up a small amount of tabletop epoxy, leaving it clear, and fill spots, if any, that have dipped below the surface of the wood. As well as filling epoxy dips, this is a great time to fill in any cracks and voids in the wood that are not filled up the whole way. Once this is done, let it cure overnight. In the morning, you can remove your table from the form!

2. Remove screws from your form's end boards. Once your table has cured overnight, you can remove it from the form. First, remove the screws securing the end boards to the plywood and, with a hammer, tap (sometimes beat) them off the end of the table.

3. Remove screws that attach the tabletop to the form and use wedges to pop the tabletop out of the form. Find some wood scraps and cut six wood wedges. Using these, place the pointed edge of the wedge between the form and the tabletop on all four corners and in the center on either side of the slabs. Then, slowly start tapping the wedge underneath the table, working your way around. Sometimes, the table will pop loose in one moment. Other times, you will hear it slowly creak and ease away from the form. Be careful you don't force the tabletop off or you risk ruining your hard work.

4. Use a planer to remove any high spots on your tabletop. Now that you have the tabletop off the form, it is time to sand it. Since you start with flattened slabs, this step is much easier than working with warped or uneven slabs. If there are any high spots from where you filled in a void with epoxy, or if your slabs have just a bit of twist, get a hand plane and take the epoxy and/or wood down to where one or two more passes with the plane would start hitting the wood. This is an excellent place to stop and will keep you from making a gouge that would take hours of sanding to remove.

5. Sand the tabletop with a handheld belt sander. Start sanding with a wide, handheld belt sander, going back and forth in line with the grain. I start with 60- or 80-grit sandpaper on a 4" (10.2cm)–wide belt. The wider the sander belt, the easier it is to keep level. When using this coarse sandpaper, make sure to keep moving; do not let the sander run too long in one spot or you will create an uneven surface quickly. Once the table is as smooth as 80 grit can make a surface, repeat the process with 100 grit until rough scratches from the 80 grit are removed. Then, move up to 120 grit, and finally, 150 grit. This will take a lot of time. Don't rush it.

6. Use an orbital sander to make make your tabletop even smoother. Make the top a bit smoother by using an orbital hand sander. Start with 80-grit sandpaper before moving on to 100, 120, and 150 grit. With your pneumatic or electric sander, slowly go back and forth, sanding in the direction of the grain, only moving up to the next grit once the previous grit scratches have been removed.

7. Fill small voids with CA glue. Most likely, you opened some small voids in the wood from sanding. Using clear CA glue, fill any voids. Slowly run the CA glue into the void, then spray the spot of glue with a CA activator. The spot will harden and be ready to sand within seconds. Using your orbital sander, sand the CA glue so it is smooth and level with the tabletop.

9. Trim your tabletop to size. For this table, I poured the width at 33" (83.8cm), and I want to finish up at 32½" (82.6cm). Take off a ¼" (6.4mm) slice of each side with your circular saw. For the length, I poured the table at 98" (249cm) but want to finish up at 96" (244cm). Using a square to measure, trim approximately 1" (2.5cm) off each end. On most tables, you would be getting very close to being done with the sanding and cutting part of the table. But, on waterfall table, we are doing something just a bit different. Before I go on to that, I will go through the steps to finish up a regular tabletop, like the coffee and end table we are making. See page 106 to continue instructions for the waterfall table.

8. Sand the bottom of your tabletop. To sand the bottom of the tabletop, use a 1" (2.5cm)–wide chisel. Scrape off the caulking beads you put on the slabs when setting them in the form. There may also be some excess epoxy that will need to be scraped off. With a handheld belt sander, smooth the epoxy between the two caulking beads. Sand this section until it is even with the wood slabs on either side.

10. Sand and rout the edges of your tabletop. Sand the edges of your table smooth with an orbital sander, removing any marks on the wood from the circular saw. Rout all the edges with a ⅛" (3.2mm) roundover bit, removing the sharp corners. Now, with a piece of 150-grit sandpaper on your belt sander, sand the routed edge, smoothing the routing cut. Keep sanding with the orbital sander by going over the top and edges again with 150-grit sandpaper. This will remove any scratches made when trimming and routing. Go over the top and edge with 220 grit, and then finish with 320 grit for an even, smooth finish!

Now, we are finally done with the sander on these two tables! Next, we will make a pair of legs and then get some oil finish on the wood and watch it come to life!

Chapter 7: Cutting, Sanding, and Machining the Tabletop

Finishing Your Waterfall Tabletop and Leg

Now, let's continue with the waterfall dining table. You want to finish up at 96" (243.8cm), but your finished tabletop will only be 60" (152.4cm), so how does that work? You will use the leftover 36" (91.4cm) as a "waterfall leg," bringing this table to a counter-height dining table. Don't be intimidated by cutting into this tabletop. As long as you're paying attention, everything will go smoothly.

1. Measure and clamp your tabletop. Measure 36" (91.4cm) from one end, marking it on either side to ensure a straight line. To cut this tabletop, get two boards that will span from the table portion of the top to the leg portion of the top and clamp them to your tabletop (see picture above). Use four clamps per side—two on the top side, and two on the leg's side. This will keep the leg stable and prevent it falling when you separate it by cutting through the entire slab.

2. Cut the leg for your waterfall table. For this cut, I recommend a track saw because the track keeps the saw gliding across the wood in a smooth, 100 percent straight line. Set your saw to 45 degrees, make a few test cuts, and confirm they form a perfect 90-degree angle together. Clamp your track to the work surface, lining up the blade on your mark, which is 36" (91.4cm) from the bottom of the leg. Angle the blade toward the bottom of the leg and start sawing. I recommend cutting in small increments, possibly a ½" (1.3cm) at a time. This keeps the blade from wandering, as most saws can't cut through 2½" (6.4cm) of hard maple in one pass. You are done cutting the leg. Set it aside.

TIP: Have someone help hold the saw base square against the tables so it does not try to tip.

3. Cut the other end of the tabletop. Make another cut on the same end of the table, now with your saw angled the opposite way. Start by cutting into the wood a depth of 1/32" to 1/16" (0.8 to 1.5mm)—just enough to remove and tear out splinters, but no more than needed. As you did for the previous cut, make several passes until you've cut a triangle-shaped piece of wood free from underneath the tabletop. This should create a perfect 45-degree joint between your two tabletop pieces.

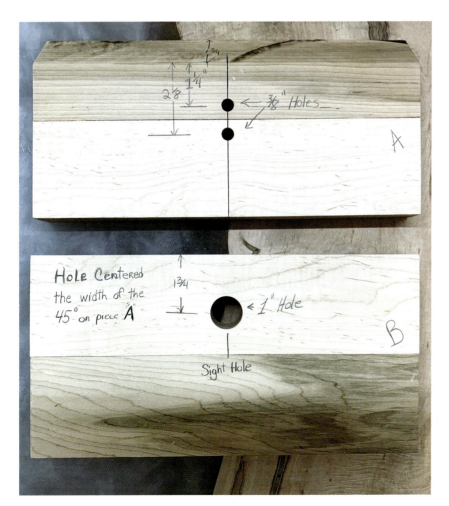

4. Cut the boards you will use to make your jig. With such a technical joint, using glue and clamps could result in the pieces sliding around. Dowels will strengthen the joint and stabilize it during glue-up! Make a jig to mark precisely where holes need to be drilled so each side lines up perfectly with the other. Use two boards, approximately 12" x 6" (30 x 15cm). Here I glued up two 3" (7.5cm) boards to get one 6" (15cm) board. These boards are 1¼" (3.2cm) thick; adjust your measurements if your boards are thicker or thinner. These will be boards A and B.

5. Cut and drill board A for your jig. For board A, cut a 45-degree angle along one edge. Using a square, tape measure, and pencil, mark the center of the board on the front and down the 45-degree slope. Drill two 3/8" (1cm) guide holes, which will keep the drill straight when you place the holes on the joint edge. Drill the first hole on the center-marked line, 1¼" (3.2cm) down from where the flat of the board meets the 45-degree cut. The second hole is also on the center-marked line, 2⅛" (5.4cm) down from where the flat of the board meets the 45-degree cut.

Chapter 7: Cutting, Sanding, and Machining the Tabletop

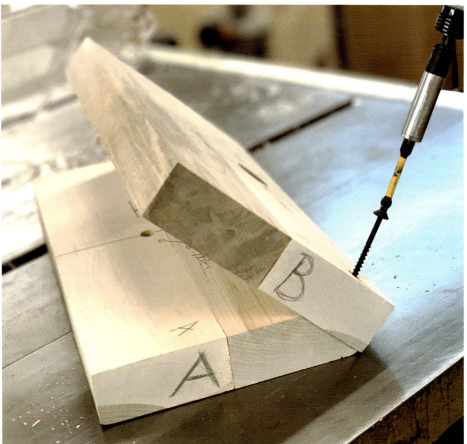

6. Drill your sight hole for board B. This will be used to align the jig with the line marks on the table joint. Use a 1" (2.5cm) drill bit to drill this hole directly in the center (when measured from end to end) and down 1¾" (4.4cm) from the top edge of the board. Cutting 1¼" (3.2cm)–thick boards on a 45-degree angle makes the surface of the cut 1¾" (4.4cm) wide.

7. Join boards A and B with screws to complete your jig. Lay B against the slope of A. Then, run two screws through B into A.

Building Wood and Resin River-Style Tables

8. Mark where your leg will meet the tabletop. Set both the leg and top pieces of the table against each other with the sharp edges touching. Make sure they are even side to side. They will be joined precisely how they are currently spaced. Using a straight edge, make a mark that goes from the leg to tabletop. Make sure there are at least two marks on either side of the river. Do not make any marks on the epoxy portion of the table.

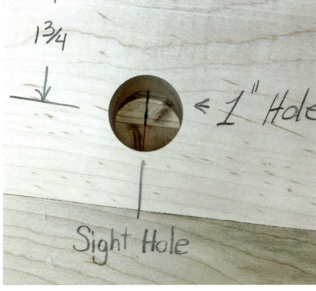

9. Line your jig up with a mark on the tabletop. Using the jig you created, set it on the joint end of the tabletop with side A on top and the sight hole facing up. Slide the jig down the joint while looking through the hole until the centerline on the jig lines up perfectly with a mark on the tabletop. Once it does, clamp it fast and double-check to ensure the lines are still lined up.

Chapter 7: Cutting, Sanding, and Machining the Tabletop

10. Drill holes where your jig lines up with the marks on your tabletop and leg. Drill a hole ⅞" (2.2cm) deep toward the thinner area of the joint. Drill another hole toward the thicker section of the joint 1" (2.5cm) deep. On a ⅜" (10mm) drill bit, use either a piece of tape or a drill bit stop to mark the depths you need. Then, drill your holes. Repeat this process on every mark you made on both edges of the joint.

11. Flip your tabletop and leg over and prepare epoxy. Now that the holes are drilled, flip both the tabletop piece and leg piece around so the holes you just drilled are facing up. Before you start gluing, mix 2–4 ounces (59.1–118.3ml) of tabletop epoxy, and have them ready to use with a brush.

12. Glue the holes and insert your pegs. Apply wood glue to the joint's surface, leaving the epoxy river section dry. Then, glue all the holes. Insert all your pegs in the holes of the tabletop side of the joint, making sure to match the longer pegs to the deeper holes. Tap them in with a hammer until they are firmly seated in the holes. Brush the epoxy mixed in step 11 on both the wood and epoxy river surfaces.

Building Wood and Resin River-Style Tables

13. Join the tabletop and leg. Now it is time to put everything back together. Pick up the leg piece and line up the holes in the leg with the pegs in the tabletop. Using a rubber mallet, tap the leg down into the joint as far as it will go.

14. Clamp the joint tight. Place several clamps so they are pulling from the joint to the bottom of the leg, and place several so they are pulling from the joint to the end of the table. Slowly and evenly tighten these until the joint is snug and the glue and epoxy are oozing out.

TIP: Before clamping, I recommend getting some cardboard, small scraps of wood, or anything else that you can position between the clamps and the surface of the wood. This will spread the pressure of the clamps out and provide a cushion that will save you from sanding clamp marks out of the wood.

Chapter 7: Cutting, Sanding, and Machining the Tabletop   111

15. Let the glue and epoxy cure. In the morning, remove the clamps. With an orbital sander, remove any glue drips and epoxy that squeezed out of the joint. You will also need to sand away any clamp marks.

16. Rout the edges of the table. Using a router with a ⅛" (3.2mm) roundover bit, rout the tops, bottoms, and corners of all the edges.

17. Sand your edges and surfaces smooth. With a piece of 80-grit sandpaper, hand-sand the roundover to smooth out the cut made by the router. Going back to the orbital sander, sand over the outer surface of the tabletop and leg again with 100-, 120-, and 150-grit sandpaper, 220 grit, and once more with 320 grit!

CHAPTER 8:
Making, Mounting, and Finishing Table Legs

Keys for Table Legs

- » You will only need to make one U-style leg for your waterfall table, as the other leg was made in Chapter 7 as an extension of the tabletop
- » U-style legs can be used on any sort of tabletop, not just those covered in this chapter
- » The Shou Sugi Ban finishing method should only be attempted outdoors
- » Follow the same process for mounting wooden legs you've built or metal legs you've purchased
- » You will not completely secure your wooden table legs to the tabletop until after you have applied the finish to your tabletop in Chapter 9

Now you can finally set the sander aside! Your tabletop is done and ready for finish. All we need to do is make some legs, and you can soon start using your table!

Tools & Materials

- Eight boards per table, except for the waterfall table, for which you'll only need four (size will vary depending on the table)
- Circular saw/track saw
- Drilling jig (see pages 107 and 108)
- Drill
- 5⁄16" (7.9mm) and ¼" (6.4mm) drill bits
- Countersink drill bit (3⁄16" [4.8mm] inside bit and 3⁄8" [10mm] main bit)
- Wood glue
- Dowels
- Screws/bolts (size will vary depending upon needs of your table)
- Natural finishing oil
- Towel

At this point in the process, your table is finally coming together. The most difficult parts are out of the way, so pat yourself on the back! In this chapter, we will cover making and mounting your table legs, as well as applying a finish to them.

Now that the sanding and sawing are done on the tabletops, you need some legs to attach to the tabletops. There are hundreds of leg styles you can make. I will show you one basic style done in two variations. For the most part, any set of legs will work for a river-style table. As long as you like it and it is the right size for your table, it should work!

Waterfall Dining Table Legs and Finish

Since you already have one leg on the waterfall table, you only need to make one more for it. This leg will be a "U" design, with two 45-degree joints like the waterfall table joint we made in Chapter 7. Make a test cut and check the angle before cutting the lumber for the legs. I will be using 3"x 1 1/4" (7.6 x 3.2cm) maple lumber.

2. Cut 45-degree angles on both ends of board A. Board A will be the section of the leg that sits against the floor. Make a 45-degree cut on the end of the board, not cutting off any more than needed. At the other end of the board, make another 45-degree cut, this time cutting the board to 28" (71.1cm) when measured from its longest points.

3. Make a 45-degree cut on one end of boards B1 and B2. Cut the boards so—when measured from the uncut end to the longest edge—the boards measure 33½" (85.1cm).

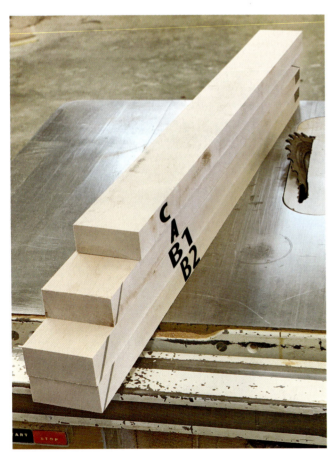

1. Cut your lumber to size. Cut your lumber into three sizes: one 29" (73.6cm) board (A), two 34" (86.4cm) boards (B1 and B2), and one 27" (68.6cm) board (C). You will not need to cut your 27" (68.6cm) board (C) again after this point, but you will need to make some cuts to the others in the following steps.

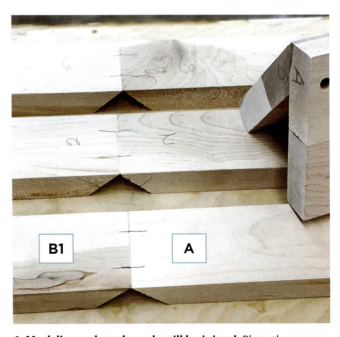

4. Mark lines where boards will be joined. Place the 45-degree joints of the boards against each other. Line them up edge to edge. Starting with B1 against A, use a straight edge to mark two lines spanning from one board to the other. On the other end of A, mark lines spanning from A to B2. We will use these marks just as we did to glue up the joint on the waterfall table (see pages 109–111).

5. Place your jig on the 45-degree cut of board A and line up with your marks. Using the jig you made in Chapter 7, clamp the board tightly and set the jig on the end with the 45-degree cut. Using the sight hole on the top, line it up with one of the marks you made and clamp it against the board.

6. Using your jig as a guide, drill holes into board A. Repeat steps 4–5 on all boards with 45-degree cuts. Now, drill a ⅜" (1cm) hole ⅝" (1.6cm) deep into the wood, only using the top guide hole in your jig. Do not drill a hole using the bottom guide hole. Adjust how deep you drill your hole depending on the thickness of the lumber you are using. Once your first hole is drilled, slide your jig over to the second mark you made and repeat. Do this on all the boards with 45-degree cuts.

7. Cut a lip into boards B1 and B2. Now, take boards B1 and B2 on the opposite ends of their 45-degree cuts. You need to cut a notch out of the inside of each board. With the board upright (standing vertically), set the table saw blade to 1¼" (3.2cm) deep. Then, lay the board down horizontally. Next, set the fence of the table so you will leave a ½" (1.3cm) lip on the outside when cut. Once this is done to both pieces, set your table saw depth until the blade meets with the saw cut you just made as illustrated in the picture above.

8. Drill countersink holes into boards B1 and B2. Next, put a combination bit in a drill or drill press to drill pilot countersink holes for screws and bolts. On B1 and B2, drill two countersink holes in the center of the lip you just cut.

Chapter 8: Making, Mounting, and Finishing Table Legs

9. Drill countersink holes into board C. On the ends of board C, drill a total of eight countersink holes, four holes on each side. Create the first row of holes 1" or 2" (2.5 or 5.1cm) from the end of the board. The second row of holes is 1" or 2" (2.5 or 5.1cm) beyond the first row. Through these holes, you will bolt the legs to the table. Sand over the flats of the boards now to get them smooth. The legs are more difficult to sand when they are all assembled.

10. Apply wood glue. The assembly process for this is very similar to the waterfall joint. Start by applying glue to the surfaces of the 45-degree cuts. Then, apply glue to the inside of the holes.

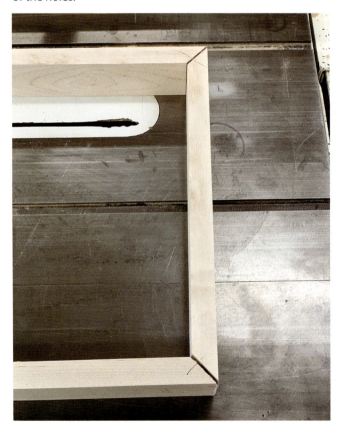

11. Insert pegs and join boards A, B1, and B2. Next, tap your pegs into the holes on boards B1 and B2. Line up the holes on board A with the pegs on B1. Start pressing the joint together. Repeat with A and B2. Once the joints are relatively tight, put a clamp on, pulling the B boards toward each other.

12. Place board C in the cutouts of B1 and B2 and join with screws. With boards B1, A, and B2 clamped together, arrange the structure so A is on the floor and the cutouts on B1 and B2 are facing up. Place board C into the cutouts. Run screws in through the countersink holes to secure C in place.

13. Clamp your boards and let glue cure overnight. Next, place a few more clamps on, pulling the joint tighter, and let it sit overnight. Be sure that your clamps are pulling from several directions to create a tight bond.

14. Remove clamps. After the glue has dried, remove the clamps. Use 80-grit sandpaper to sand the outside flats and remove any glue drips.

15. Rout and sand all edges. Rout all the edges with the 1/8" (3.2mm) roundover bit. Once that is done, use a piece of 80-grit sandpaper to smooth the routed edges.

16. Apply finish. For the finish on these legs, add a natural oil just like you will do on the tabletops. I recommend using a Polyx-Oil that hardens and does not wear down. Put some oil on a towel and wipe it over all the surfaces. Then, take a dry towel and buff it dry. After eight hours, repeat, and you are done.

Ocean End Table Legs and Finish

We will use the same tools and materials to build the end table legs as we used for the U-style waterfall table legs. The process is almost the same, though there are a few differences. We will be doing a different type of finish for the end table. The technique is called Shou Sugi Ban, an ancient Japanese method that preserves the wood by charring its surface with fire. The wood will also be finished with oil. This makes the wood much more durable and resistant to moisture. Please note that you will need to construct two U-style legs for your end table.

The best place to do this finish will be outside in the open. Do not have an open flame around any wood or other flammable item other than the product you are burning. Keep a bucket of water or fire extinguisher on hand just in case something does not go as planned.

1. Construct U-style legs. For construction of the end table legs, follow steps 1–15 of the U-style legs in the previous section. For board A, we will cut it to 20" (50.8cm). For the boards B1 and B2, we will cut them to 28" (71.1cm). For board C, we will cut them to 19" (48.3cm). All these measurements can be adjusted to fit your vision for your table. Once built, it is time to apply our finish.

When using the Shou Sugi Ban finishing method, there are additional safety measures to keep in mind.

- The best place to perform the Shou Sugi Ban finishing method is outside in the open.
- Do not have an open flame around any wood or other flammable item other than the product you are burning.
- Keep a bucket of water or fire extinguisher on hand just in case something does not go as planned.

2. Char your table legs with a propane torch. Using a propane torch, turn the temperature to medium/high and slowly start running the flame across the wood, watching it turn a deep brown or black. Your torch should be close enough for the flame to lightly touch the surface of the wood. Make sure to keep moving and not stay at one spot too long. Do this on all the wood surfaces until it is evenly charred.

3. Remove excess carbon from wood's surface. Once the wood is cool enough to touch, attach a wire brush to a drill and run it across all the charred wood surfaces. This will remove the excess carbon left behind from the burning and give the wood a unique texture.

4. Apply oil to the table legs. When you are finished wire-brushing, wipe off all the dust. Apply a liberal amount of Polyx-Oil to the whole surface of the leg with a towel. Once the legs are all covered, use a dry towel to buff dry. Let the oil cure for eight hours and repeat. You have just completed the Shou Sugi Ban technique!

Mounting Your Table Legs

For the coffee table, I will be buying a set of metal legs from a small business that manufactures them, and I highly recommend that you do the same for some of your future projects. You can find these shops all over the USA. Most likely, a metal fabrication shop in your town would be glad to make you a set. This is a great way to support local small businesses. Since you do not have to go through all the steps of making the legs, I will show you how to mount the legs to the bottom of the tabletop. This process will apply to all the legs in this chapter: handmade wooden legs or metal legs you bought.

1. Space your table legs out equally and mark your mounting holes. Lay your tabletop upside down. Make sure to spread some towels or foam between the tabletop and where it is resting so the top is not marred. For the metal legs, set them on the table bottom and use a tape measure to space them out equally from side to side and end to end. Now that the legs are set how you want them mounted, trace the mounting holes with a pencil onto the bottom of the table.

You can purchase metal legs from a local fabrication shop.

2. Place wooden legs where you want to attached them to the tabletop and mark holes. For the wooden legs, arrange them where you want them attached to the bottom of your chosen tabletop. Take the drill bit used to drill the mounting holes and insert it into all the holes in the leg. Press down firmly on the tabletop. This will leave a mark in the exact center of each hole that you will use as a guide.

Building Wood and Resin River-Style Tables

3. Drill your mounting holes. Now that you know where to drill the holes, get a drill bit. For the inserts I am using for the coffee table legs, the manufacturers recommend using a 5/16" (7.9mm) drill bit. Set the point of the drill bit in the center of your markings and drill a hole straight down into your table. My inserts are ¾" (1.9cm) long, so I will be drilling the holes ⅞" (2.2cm) deep to give a bit of wiggle room. Mark the depth on the bit or put a stop on the bit. You do not want to drill through to the surface of the table! While these specific measurements apply to my purchased coffee table legs, the overall process detailed in this step applies to both metal legs and the wooden legs we have made in this chapter.

4. Use rotary burr to create a bevel. Once you have all the holes drilled, place a rotary burr in the center of the hole. Run the drill until the burr cuts a 1/16"–1/8" (1.6–3.2mm) bevel. This will get the inserts started and help them sit flush with the surface.

5. Install your metal inserts. Install your metal inserts with an Allen wrench to tighten them into the hole. Screw these down into the hole until they are flush with the tabletop. The final steps to mount the legs happens after you add finish to the tabletop! I recommend setting the legs on the table and starting a bolt into all your inserts to make sure everything is perfectly square and level before finishing up the tabletop and bottom.

TIP: If the placement of your legs means you need to put an insert where there is epoxy, heat the insert up with a torch so it "melts" the epoxy as it is threaded into it. If you do not do this, it can strip out the hole.

Chapter 8: Making, Mounting, and Finishing Table Legs

CHAPTER 9:
Finishing the Tabletop

Keys to Finishing Your Tabletops

- » Wear gloves when applying oil
- » Natural oils are great to showcase the wood grain in your tabletops
- » Apply oil evenly and within the same time frame to prevent warping and discoloration
- » Finish securing your table legs to the tabletop after you have applied your finish to the tabletop

You have reached the homerun stretch! This table is just about ready to be put to use.

Tools & Materials

- Gloves
- Natural finishing oil
- Super polish scrubbing pad
- Towel
- Sandpaper (grit will vary based upon need)
- Orbital sander

Congratulations! You are almost finished with your one-of-a-kind river-style table. With just a few finishing touches, you will be completely done. In this chapter, we will cover applying a finish to your table and fully securing your table legs.

It is time for one of the most enjoyable processes of making the table: putting the finish on and watching the wood come to life! In this chapter, I will be using a Polyx-Oil for the finish. Many of their finishes would work, as well as many types of oil finishes in general. I recommend a natural oil such as tung or linseed oil to show off the wood grain to its best effect. Make sure to follow the directions of the exact finish you are using. The steps here are generally the same for most oil finishes.

1. Wipe dust from tabletop and apply oil. To start, wipe all the dust off the tabletop. Wear gloves because oil finishes don't just wash off your hands like dirt! It's easiest to finish the bottom first. To apply the oil, we will use a super polish scrubbing pad. Pour some oil onto your pad or tabletop and start spreading it across the surface. Only add more oil when the oil is all rubbed in. Do this until the bottom of the table is completely covered. Then buff the excess oil off with a dry towel. Let this sit for a few minutes. Don't wait until the oil has cured; the uneven application of oil from the bottom to the top of the table could cause the wood to warp.

2. Sand away any scratches and apply more oil. After a few minutes, flip the tabletop over. Check for any marks on the surface of the tabletop and sand them out before applying the oil. Repeat the oiling process on the top. Instead of wiping the oil off with a dry towel, use a pad like the one you are using to apply the oil. This will leave a bit more oil on the surface and give it a glossier sheen.

Chapter 9: Finishing the Tabletop

3. Buff the oil on the tabletop and let it cure. After the table is completely covered in oil, rub a thin layer of oil on the surface of a dry pad. A completely dry pad can remove oil. Then, start buffing the surface until most of the oil has been worked into the wood. To speed up this process, cut a sheet of your buffing pad into a square and place it on your orbital sander. You will need a sander with a hook-and-loop pad for this to attach. Then, running the sander on medium to slow speed, slowly go back and forth, buffing the oil until the table has an even sheen. Let the table cure for eight hours.

4. After oil cures, buff it again as in previous step. When the first cure is done, repeat the exact same process as step 3. Your tabletop is done! Most oils recommend letting the finish cure for a week before use, so we do not want to rush anything at this point. Some oil finishes require sanding between coats, so be sure to check your oil brand specifications.

5. Secure your table legs to the tabletop. Once the finish is fully cured, flip the tabletop around for mounting the legs. Line up the holes in the legs with the inserts secured into the bottom of the tabletop and thread your bolts in. Use bolts with the same diameter and thread type as required for the inserts. Tighten the bolts down. Your legs are now secured to your table!

You are now completely finished with your one-of-a-kind river-style table!

Get a friend to help you flip the table over. Now you are completely done! Take a moment to pat yourself on the back! You have a one-of-a-kind table that you made from scratch. With the skills and techniques used in making your tabletop, you can now make many things—cutting boards, charcuterie boards, wall art, desks, cabinet tops . . . and the list could go on!

WATERFALL DINING TABLE

OCEAN END TABLE

ROCKY RIVER COFFEE TABLE

Chapter 9: Finishing the Tabletop

About the Author

Bradlyn Zimmerman started his business, TheOleWoodShack, as a side hobby in his dad's woodshop. He and his father made handcrafted wood chairs for his uncle's wholesale furniture company. In the early 2010s, they started making a few live edge tables for his company. There, father and son learned some of the tricks and tips to making live edge tables through research and trial and error. When making live edge tables, there were always scrap cutoffs; Bradlyn turned the cutoffs into floating shelves and other small pieces and sold them. He called this side hobby "TheOleWoodShack." After a few years, he made a few live edge river-style tables on the side and sold them directly to clients. From there, this hobby turned into a business! Between making chairs and tables, Bradlyn and his dad are kept busy, and he considers it a pleasure to make useful pieces of art for their clients.

The author and his dad delivering a table to a client.

PHOTO CREDITS

Front Cover: *background banner* Alter Ego Art/Shutterstock.com; *top table* Pavel Vaschenkov/Shutterstock.com; *bottom right* Suteren/Shutterstock.com **Page 2:** *wood background* FusionStudio/Shutterstock.com **Page 4:** *wood and resin banner* FusionStudio/Shutterstock.com; *pouring resin* Suteren/Shutterstock.com **Page 5:** *background* Suteren/Shutterstock.com; *top middle* Bekker24/Shutterstock.com **Pages 6–7:** *background* Sentelia/Shutterstock.com **Pages 10–31:** Bradlyn Zimmerman, TheOleWoodShack **Pages 32–33:** Christopher Forcenito, Cf Woodworks Llc **Pages 34–36:** David Shaw, The Northern Joinery **Pages 37–50:** Ibrahim Guler, Artist and Founder Of Jehoel's Work **Pages 51–54:** Kyle and Ali Johnson, Backwoods Timber Creations **Pages 55–57:** Lindsay Russell, Backwood Design Co. **Pages 58–60:** Nick Demao, Woodeyes Woodworks **Pages 61–64:** Nick Hunter, Hunter Edge Woodworks **Page 65:** Rachel Walker-Hook, Chessie Goes Wild Art **Page 66:** *bandsaw, circular saw, orbital sander* OlegSam/Shutterstock.com; *tape measure* B Calkins/Shutterstock.com; *sandpaper* Jiang Zhongyan/Shutterstock.com **Page 67:** *grinding bits* Praethip Docekalova/Shutterstock.com; *chisel* agolndr/Shutterstock.com; *rotary tool* Siarhei Kuranets/Shutterstock.com; *wire wheel brushes* Phichai/Shutterstock.com; *abrasive wheels* Weblogiq/Shutterstock.com; *drill* OlegSam/Shutterstock.com; *screwdriver* Stakon/Shutterstock.com; *hammer* VRVIRUS/Shutterstock.com; *caulking gun* janniwet/Shutterstock.com **Page 68:** *hairdryer* cristi180884/Shutterstock.com; *box fan* focal point/Shutterstock.com; *power planer* Aleksey Dushutin/Shutterstock.com; *c-clamp* Amnartk/Shutterstock.com; *router* stockphoto-graf/Shutterstock.com; *f-clamps* Irina Rogova/Shutterstock.com; *propane torch* crotonoil/Shutterstock.com **Page 69:** *shells and rocks* TADDEUS/Shutterstock.com; *screws* Bingo TB/Shutterstock.com; *syringe* vilax/Shutterstock.com; *gloves* Florin Burlan/Shutterstock.com **Page 70:** Marco Zamperini/Shutterstock.com **Page 71:** Valentyn Volkov/Shutterstock.com **Page 119:** *top right* Alessandro Narciso/Shutterstock.com **Back Cover:** *background banner* Alter Ego Art/Shutterstock.com; *bottom left* Sentelia/Shutterstock.com

Index

Note: Page references in parentheses indicate intermittent references.

A
abrasive wheels, 67
adhesives, 68, 69

B
beech table, Pittsburgh Steel, 18
black walnut. *See* walnut tables
boards, 69
bolts, 69
brush, for epoxy, 68
brush, wire wheel, 67
Buckeye Burl, 27
burr, rotary/carbide, 67

C
caulking gun/caulk, 67
cedar tables
 Berkshire Table, 10
 Cedar Kitchenette, 26
chisel, 67
clamps, 68
coffee tables, 25, (53–55), 57, 62, 64, 73, 83, 89, 97–98, 120–21, 125
color additive, 69
color additive, adding to epoxy, 94
Cottonwood California, 28
credenzas, 20, 34, 45
cypress, Pecky Table, 60

D
dowels/pegs, 69
drill, drill bits, drilling jig, 67
dust collector, 69

E
English Elm, 16, 60
epoxy
 examples of coloring methods used (*See* gallery of tables)
 pouring (*See* pouring river-style tables)
 preparing and coloring, 90–92
 readying for pouring, 77–83
 types of, 69
epoxy tables
 Churning End Table, 49
 Ocean Waves, 37

F
fan, 68
finishing tabletop. *See* preparing tabletop
forms, epoxy table
 buying prebuilt, 69
 making, 84–89
 materials for, 69

G
gallery of tables
 DeMao, Nick (WoodEyes Woodworks), 58–60
  English Elm, 60
  Hunter Green Table, 58
  Pecky Table, 60
  Spalted Maple Table, 59
 Forcenito, Christopher (CFWoodworksLLC), 32–33
  Baja Blue, 33
  English Walnut Swirl, 33
  Maple Dining Table, 32
 Guler, Ibrahim (Jehoel's Works), 37–50
  Blue River-Style Table, 44
  Cast Wood, 48
  Churning End Table, 49
  Colorful Epoxy Table, 38
  Dark Waters, 44
  Dining Table with Silver Base, 50
  Envy Green, 46
  Floating Driftwood, 41
  Forking River, 42
  Industrial Table, 47
  Island Oasis, 40
  King's Table, 49
  Knotty Table, 48
  Lightning Strike, 45
  Minimalist Table, 42
  Ocean Waves, 37
  Onyx, 47
  Placid River, 48
  Realistic River, 40
  Shore Table, 39
  Spalted Dark Hardwood, 43
 Hunter, Nick (Hunter Edge Woodworks), 61–64
  Black Walnut Dining Table, 63
  Blue Streak, 61
  Galaxy Table, 64
  Game On, 62
  Small Coffee Table, 62
  Spalted Maple Coffee Table, 64
  Walnut End Table, 62
 John, Kyle & Ali (Backwoods Timber Creations), 51–54
  Maple Burl Coffee Table, 53
  Spalted Maple Table, 51
  Swirling River, 52
  Tundra Table, 52
  Walnut Coffee Table, 54
 Russell, Lindsay (Backwood Design Co.), 55–57
  Black Walnut Set, 55
  Peninsula Table, 56
  Round Walnut Table, 57
  Sugar Maple Table, 57
 Shaw, David (The Northern Journey), 34–36
  Black and Gold Table, 36
  Mappa Burl Vanity, 35
  Spalted Maple Credenza, 34
 Walker-Hook, Rachel (Chessie Goes Wild ART)
  Ocean Table, 65
 Zimmerman, Bradlyn (TheOleWoodShack), 10–31
  Anderson Gray, 17
  Beach House Maple, 28
  Berkshire Table, 10
  Black Onyx, 14
  Black Walnut Coffee Table, 25
  Buckeye Girl, 27
  Cedar Kitchenette, 26
  Claro Walnut Credenza, 20
  Classic Chic, 26
  Cottonwood California, 28
  Englander, 15
  English Elm, 16
  Figured Maple Ice, 19
  Green Emerald, 21
  Jackson Teal, 14
  Lava Canyon, 24
  Mappa Coffee, 19
  Marble Claro, 24
  Misty Blues, 12
  Nokon Walnut, 23
  Ocean Shores, 30
  Pacifica, 13
  Pittsburgh Steel, 18
  Quilted Maple, 29
  Seashell Cove, 30
  Southern Dining, 27
  Stoney Brook, 31
  Texas Maple, 16
  Triangle Black Walnut, 22
  Vegas Mesa, 11
  Vibrant Blue, 18
  Walnut Beam, 21
  Walnut Trestle, 31
  Walnut Waves, 23
  Welke Walnut, 14
  White Waterfalls, 25
gloves, 69
glue, CA, 68

H
hairdryer, 68
hammer, 67
hardwoods. *See also* specific hardwoods
 Blue River-Style Table, 44
 Cast Wood, 48
 Colorful Epoxy Table, 38

Dark Waters, 44
Dining Table with Silver Base, 50
Envy Green, 46
Forking River, 42
Industrial Table, 47
Island Oasis, 40
King's Table, 49
Knotty Table, 48
Lightning Strike, 45
Minimalist Table, 42
Onyx, 47
Placid River, 48
Realistic River, 40
Shore Table, 39
Spalted Dark Hardwood, 43
Swirling River, 52

K
kitchenette, 26

L
legs
  constructing U-style legs, 114–15, 119
  construction examples (*See* gallery of tables)
  finishing waterfall tabletop and leg, 106–12
  keys for table legs, 113
  making, mounting, and finishing, 113–21
  mounting, 120–21
  waterfall table legs and finish, 114–18
live edge furniture
  history and book overview, 72–73
  preparing for pouring epoxy, 77–83
  selecting slabs for, 74–76

M
maple tables
  Beach House Maple, 28
  Black and Gold Table, 36
  Blue Streak, 61
  Classic Chic, 26
  Figured Maple Ice, 19
  Hunter Green Table, 58
  Maple Burl Coffee Table, 53
  Maple Dining Table, 32
  Misty Blues, 12
  Ocean Shores, 30
  Ocean Table, 65
  Pacifica, 13
  Quilted Maple, 29
  Seashell Cove, 30
  Southern Dining, 27
  Spalted Maple Coffee Table, 64
  Spalted Maple Credenza, 34
  Spalted Maple Table, 51, 59
  Sugar Maple Table, 57
  Texas Maple, 16
  Tundra Table, 52
  Vibrant Blue, 18

White Waterfalls, 25
mappa tables, 19, 35
materials and safety, 69
measuring/marking tools, 66
melamine or plywood, 69
mixing, tools for, 68

O
objects, to embed, 69
ocean end table
  completed example, photo, 125
  constructing U-style legs, 114–15, 119
  finishing tabletop, 122–25
  legs and finish, 119–20
  mounting legs, 120–21
  pouring, 99–101
  Shou Sugi Ban finishing method, 119–20
oil, applying to table, 123–24
olive wood, Floating Driftwood, 41
overview of building river-style tables, 8–9

P
pegs/dowels, 69
planer, power, 68
plywood or melamine, 69
pouring river-style tables, 93–101
  avoiding/popping bubbles, 93, (94–96)
  checking for leaks in form, 95
  classic river-style pour, 93–96
  letting epoxy cure, 95
  ocean end table pour, 99–101
  rocky river coffee table pour, 97–98
  second pour, 97
  swirling epoxy as cures, 96
preparing tabletop. *See also* pouring river-style tables
  cutting, sanding, and machining, 102–12
  finishing tabletop (after curing), 103–5
  finishing tabletop (final), 122–25
  finishing waterfall tabletop and leg, 106–12
propane torch, 68

R
river-style tables
  forms for (*See* forms, epoxy table)
  overview of building, 8–9
  pouring (*See* pouring river-style tables)
  this book and, 6, 73
rocks and shells, 69
rocky river coffee table pour, 97–98
rotary burr, 67
rotary tool, 67
router and bits, 68

S
safety precautions, 70
sanders and sandpaper, 66. *See also* abrasive wheels

sanding techniques, 79, 96, 102, 103, 105, 112, 123–24
saw, circular, 66
screwdriver, 67
screws, 69
scrubbing pads, super polish, 69
shells and rocks, 69
Shou Sugi Ban finishing method, 119–20
spokeshave, 68
syringe, 69

T
tools and safety, 66–69, 70
towels, 69

V
vanity, mappa burl, 35

W
walnut tables
  Anderson Gray, 17
  Baja Blue, 33
  Black Onyx, 14
  Black Walnut Coffee Table, 25
  Black Walnut Dining Table, 63
  Black Walnut Set, 55
  Claro Walnut Credenza, 20
  Englander, 15
  English Walnut Swirl, 33
  Galaxy Table, 64
  Game On, 62
  Green Emerald, 21
  Jackson Teal, 14
  Lava Canyon, 24
  Marble Claro, 24
  Nokon Walnut, 23
  Peninsula Table, 56
  Round Walnut Table, 57
  Small Coffee Table, 62
  Stoney Brook, 31
  Triangle Black Walnut, 22
  Vegas Mesa, 11
  Walnut Beam, 21
  Walnut Coffee Table, 54
  Walnut End Table, 62
  Walnut Trestle, 31
  Walnut Waves, 23
  Welke Walnut, 14
waterfall table
  example (White Waterfalls), 25, 125
  finishing tabletop and leg, 106–12
  legs (cutting, mounting, finishing), 114–18
  slab leg example, photo, 73
wire wheel brush, 67
wood scraps, 69
wood species, gallery examples by. *See* specific wood species